PALGRAVE CASEBOOK SERIES (ed Anna Sandeman)

CASEBOOK SERIES

JANE AUSTEN: *'Northanger Abbey' & 'Persuasion'* B.C. Southam
JANE AUSTEN: *'Sense and Sensibility', 'Pride and Prejudice' & 'Mansfield Park'* B. C. Southam
BECKETT: *Waiting for Godot* Ruby Cohn
WILLIAM BLAKE: *Songs of Innocence and Experience* Margaret Bottrall
CHARLOTTE BRONTE: *'Jane Eyre' & 'Villette'* Miriam Allott
EMILY BRONTE: *Wuthering Heights* (Revised) Miriam Allott
BROWNING: *'Men and Women' & Other Poems* J. R. Watson
CHAUCER: *The Canterbury Tales* J. J. Anderson
COLERIDGE: *'The Ancient Mariner' & Other Poems* Alun R. Jones & W. Tydeman
CONRAD: *' Heart of Darkness', 'Nostromo' & 'Under Western Eyes'* C. B. Cox
DICKENS: *Bleak House* A. E. Dyson
DICKENS: *'Hard Times', 'Great Expectations' & 'Our Mutual Friend''* Norman Page
DONNE: *Songs and Sonnets* Julian Lovelock
GEORGE ELIOT: *Middlemarch* Patrick Swinden
T.S. ELIOT: *Four Quartets*
T.S. ELIOT: *'Prufrock', 'Gerontion' & 'Ash Wednesday'* B. C. Southam
T.S. ELIOT: *The Waste Land* C. B. Cox & Arnold P. Hinchliffe
HENRY FIELDING: *Tom Jones* Neil Compton
E.M. FORSTER: *A Passage to India* Malcolm Bradbury
HARDY: *The Tragic Novels* (Revised) R. P. Draper
HARDY: *Poems* James Gibson & Trevor Johnson
GERARD MANLEY HOPKINS: *Poems* Margaret Bottrall
HENRY JAMES: *'Washington Square' & 'The Portrait of a Lady'* Alan Shelton
JONSON: *Volpone* Jonas A. Barish
JAMES JOYCE: *'Dubliners' & 'A Portrait of the Artist as a Young Man'* Morris Beja
KEATS: *Odes* G. S. Fraser
KEATS: *Narrative Poems* John Spencer Hill
D.H. LAWRENCE: *Sons and Lovers* Gamini Salgado
D.H. LAWRENCE: *'The Rainbow' & 'Women in Love'* Colin Clarke
LOWRY: *Under the Volcano* Gordon Bowker
MARLOWE: *Doctor Faustus* John Jump
MARLOWE: *'Tamburlaine the Great', 'Edward II' & 'The Jew of Malta'* J. R. Brown
MILTON: *Paradise Lost* A.E. Dyson & Julian Lovelock
O'CASEY: *'Juno and the Paycock', 'The Plough and the Stars' & 'The Shadow of a Gunman'* Ronald Ayling
JOHN OSBORNE: *Look Back in Anger* John Russell Taylor
PINTER: *'The Birthday Party' & Other Plays* Michael Scott
POPE: *The Rape of the Lock* John Dixon Hunt
SHAKESPEARE: *A Midsummer Night's Dream* Antony Price
SHAKESPEARE: *Antony and Cleopatra* (Revised) John Russell Brown
SHAKESPEARE: *Coriolanus* B. A. Brockman

SHAKESPEARE: *Early Tragedies* Neil Taylor & Bryan Loughrey
SHAKESPEARE: *Hamlet* John Jump
SHAKESPEARE: *Henry IV Parts I and II* G. K. Hunter
SHAKESPEARE: *Henry V* Michael Quinn
SHAKESPEARE: *Julius Caesar* Peter Ure
SHAKESPEARE: *King Lear* (Revised) Frank Kermode
SHAKESPEARE: *Macbeth* (Revised) John Wain
SHAKESPEARE: *Measure for Measure* C. K. Stead
SHAKESPEARE: *The Merchant of Venice* John Wilders
SHAKESPEARE: *'Much Ado About Nothing' & 'As You Like It'* John Russell Brown
SHAKESPEARE: *Othello* (Revised) John Wain
SHAKESPEARE: *Richard II* Nicholas Brooke
SHAKESPEARE: *The Sonnets* Peter Jones
SHAKESPEARE: *The Tempest* (Revised) D. J. Palmer
SHAKESPEARE: *Twelfth Night* D. J. Palmer
SHAKESPEARE: *The Winter's Tale* Kenneth Muir
SPENSER: *The Faerie Queene* Peter Bayley
SHERIDAN: *Comedies* Peter Davison
STOPPARD: *'Rosencrantz and Guildenstern are Dead', 'Jumpers' & 'Travesties'* T. Bareham
SWIFT: *Gulliver's Travels* Richard Gravil
SYNGE: *Four Plays* Ronald Ayling
THACKERAY: *Vanity Fair* Arthur Pollard
WEBSTER: *'The White Devil' & 'The Duchess of Malfi'* R.V. Holdsworth
WILDE: *Comedies* William Tydeman
VIRGINIA WOOLF: *To the Lighthouse* Morris Beja
WORDSWORTH: *Lyrical Ballads* Alun R. Jones & William Tydeman
WORDSWORTH: *The Prelude* W. J. Harvey & Richard Gravil
YEATS: *Poems 1919-35* Elizabeth Cullingford
YEATS: *Last Poems* Jon Stallworthy

Issues in Contemporary Critical Theory Peter Barry
Thirties Poets: 'The Auden Group' Ronald Carter
Tragedy: Developments in Criticism R. P. Draper
Three Contemporary Poets: Gunn, Hughes, Thomas A. E. Dyson
The Metaphysical Poets Gerald Hammond
Medieval English Drama Peter Happé
The English Novel: Developments in Criticism since Henry James Stephen Hazell
Poetry of the First World War Dominic Hibberd
The Romantic Imagination John Spencer Hill
Drama Criticism: Developments since Ibsen Arnold P. Hinchliffe
Three Jacobean Revenge Tragedies R. V. Holdsworth
The Language of Literature Norman Page
Comedy: Developments in Criticism D. J. Palmer
Studying Shakespeare John Russell Brown
The Gothic Novel Victor Sage
Pre-Romantic Poetry J. R. Watson

John Keats

Odes

A CASEBOOK

EDITED BY

G. S. FRASER

BLOOMSBURY

NEW DELHI • LONDON • OXFORD • NEW YORK • SYDNEY

BLOOMSBURY INDIA
Bloomsbury Publishing India Pvt. Ltd
Second Floor, LSC Building No. 4, DDA Complex, Pocket C–6&7,
Vasant Kunj, New Delhi 110070

BLOOMSBURY, BLOOMSBURY ACADEMIC INDIA and the Diana logo are trademarks of Bloomsbury Publishing Plc

First published in India 2024

This edition published with permission from Bloomsbury Publishing Plc,
50 Bedford Square, London, WC1B3DP, UK

A catalogue record for this book is available from the British Library.
A catalog record for this book is available from the Library of Congress.

ISBN: 978-93-61310-00-3
For sale in the Indian subcontinent only

Printed at Manipal Technologies Limited, Manipal

CONTENTS

ACKNOWLEDGEMENTS

G. M. Hopkins, extract from *The Correspondence of G. M. Hopkins and R. W. Dixon*, ed. Claude Collier Abbott (Oxford University Press); H. W. Garrod, 'The Close Connections of Thought in the Spring Odes', from *Keats: Lectures from the Oxford Chair of Poetry* (Clarendon Press); M. R. Ridley, 'The Composition of "Nightingale"' and 'The Odes and the Sonnet Form', from *Keats's Craftsmanship: A Study in Poetic Development* (M. R. Ridley); Kenneth Burke, 'Symbolic Action in a Poem by Keats', from *A Grammar of Motives* (Prentice-Hall Inc., © Kenneth Burke 1945); G. St Quintin, 'The Grecian Urn', from *The Times Literary Supplement* (5 Feb 1938) (G. St Quintin); Alvin Whitley, 'The Message of the Grecian Urn', from *Keats–Shelley Memorial Bulletin* (1953) (Alvin Whitley); I. A. Richards, extract from *Practical Criticism* (Routledge & Kegan Paul Ltd and Harcourt, Brace, Jovanovich Inc.); I. A. Richards, extract from *Mencius on the Mind* (Routledge & Kegan Paul Ltd and Humanities Press Inc.); T. S. Eliot, extract from *Selected Essays* (Faber & Faber Ltd and Harcourt, Brace, Jovanovich Inc.); William Empson, extract from *The Structure of Complex Words* (Chatto & Windus Ltd and New Directions Inc.); Cleanth Brooks, 'Keats's Sylvan Historian', from *The Well-Wrought Urn* (Dennis Dobson and Harcourt, Brace, Jovanovich Inc.); William Empson, 'The Ambiguity of "Melancholy"', from *Seven Types of Ambiguity* (Chatto & Windus Ltd and New Directions Inc.); Allen Tate, 'A Reading of Keats', from *On the Limits of Poetry* (Swallow Press Inc.); John Holloway, 'The Odes of Keats', from *The Charted Mirror* (Routledge & Kegan Paul Ltd and Horizon Press Inc.); Leonard Unger, 'Keats and the Music of Autumn', from *The Man in the Name: Essays on the Experience of Poetry* (University of Minnesota Press, © University of Minnesota 1956); Kenneth Allott, 'The "Ode to Psyche"', from *John Keats: A Reassessment*, ed. K. Muir (Liverpool University Press); Kenneth Muir, 'The Meaning of the Odes', from *John Keats: A Reassessment* (Liverpool University Press).

INTRODUCTION

I

Keats wrote a number of poems other than those with which this book is concerned, to which he gave the title 'ode' and to one of the greatest of the poems with which this book is concerned, 'To Autumn', he (or the publishers of his 1820 volume) did not give that title. But when Swinburne, the first critic to call attention to the pre-eminent place of these poems in Keats's work, talked of 'his unequalled and unrivalled odes', he had in mind five poems which were first collected in Keats's third and by far his greatest volume, *Lamia, Isabella, The Eve of St Agnes, and Other Poems,* printed for Taylor and Hessey, Keats's friends and publishers, in July 1820. The title of this volume calls attention to the narrative poems in it, and it also contains the unfinished fragment of an epic, *Hyperion.* Narrative poetry was still thought, in 1820, a grander and more ambitious kind of poetry than the short lyric, and the most perceptive and sympathetic of the early reviewers, Charles Lamb, concentrates on the story poems and does not mention the five great odes. These are, in the order in which they appear in the volume, 'Ode to a Nightingale', 'Ode on a Grecian Urn', 'Ode to Psyche', 'To Autumn' and 'Ode on Melancholy'.

The order of composition was different. 'Psyche', 'Nightingale', 'Urn' and 'Melancholy' (for convenience I shall use these short titles from now on) were all composed between the end of April and the end of May 1819. A fifth spring ode, 'An Ode on Indolence', was not included in the 1820 volume and was first published (along with the fine fragment of an ode to Maia composed in May 1818) twenty-seven years after Keats's death by Lord Houghton, then Richard Monckton Milnes, in his *Life, Letters and Literary Remains of John Keats.* There is a puzzle about the date of its composition. Keats sketches out the circumstances and the mood which gave rise to it, and the three allegorical figures presented in it, in a letter of March 1819. In a letter of June, however, he speaks of it as the thing he has most enjoyed writing 'this year'. It is full of what might be either echoes or anticipations of the other spring odes, it does not equal (or, since it is essentially a humorous poem, attempt to equal) their elevation and intensity. We know, however, from the March letter that the mood of ironic disillusionment with poetry which it expresses preceded, not succeeded, the composition of the greater spring odes. 'To Autumn' was composed in September 1819 and differs from the spring odes in its impersonal serenity.

An ode is traditionally, in the useful definition of Babette Deutsch in her *Poetry Handbook*, 'a lyric that is exalted or enthusiastic in tone and, whether regular or not, elaborately designed'. There are two main classical sources for the form, Pindar and Horace. Pindar wrote regular odes consisting of a strophe and antistrophe, of the same form, followed by an epode of a different form; the pattern could be repeated. Gray and Collins wrote regular Pindaric odes, but in the seventeenth century Cowley and Dryden had not seen that the Pindaric ode was regular, and had created the English irregular ode, of lines and stanzas of various length; Wordsworth's Immortality ode, which Keats knew well, is probably the greatest English irregular ode, and Keats's 'Psyche' is irregular in this sense. The Horatian ode consisted of a sequence of regular strophes, and all Keats's odes except 'Psyche' are regular in this sense. Some devices of rhetoric, notably invocation and personification, he owes most directly, nevertheless, to the Pindaric style of Gray and Collins, the two poets nearest to him in time who had done their main work in the ode form.

The stanza forms of Keats's odes, except the irregular 'Psyche', are of his own invention. H. W. Garrod and M. R. Ridley have demonstrated that these forms spring from Keats's dissatisfaction with the sonnet form, or rather with his own achievement in it. The fragment of a May ode of 1818 consists of fourteen lines, showing Keats still in the grip of the sonnet form but trying, by shortening some of his line lengths, and avoiding the rhyme sequence of either a Shakespearean or a Petrarchan sonnet, to break away from it. 'Nightingale', 'Urn', 'Melancholy' and 'Indolence' are written in a ten-line stanza, consisting of the quatrain of a Shakespearean sonnet followed by the sestet of a Petrarchan sonnet; this derivation is a little disguised in 'Nightingale' by the substitution of a trimeter for a pentameter in the third last line. 'To Autumn' has an eleven-line stanza, the Petrarchan sestet becoming a septet, with a couplet, catching on to an earlier rhyme-word, just before the last line. These ten- and eleven-line stanzas are long enough to express a complex modulation of thought and feeling but not so long as to run the risk of becoming, like a sonnet in a sonnet sequence, isolated poems in themselves. 'Psyche' stands apart from the other odes in this as in other ways, but it is possible to find what might be called sonnet units in its irregular sections.

Keats thus, in all but one of the odes, had solved the problem of combining richness in the component parts of a thoughtful and elaborate lyrical poem with flow and continuity through the whole. Matthew Arnold was to adopt a variation of Keats's ode stanza, putting a Petrarchan sestet first and ending with a Petrarchan not a Shakespearean quatrain, in the two most Keatsian of his poems, 'Thyrsis' and 'The Scholar Gypsy'.

It is not pedantic to dwell on such questions. Whether or not it is true, in the words of Marshall McLuhan, that 'the medium is the message', it is often true in poetry that the form is the mood or the tone; and for a new mood or tone Keats needed to devise a new form that would yet have rich echoes of old ones. The influence on him of Gray and Collins, his most distinguished recent predecessors in the handling of the ode, is a superficial one; the influence of Shakespeare's sonnets, in their erotic evocation of spring and autumn weather, in their combination of formal beauty and opulence of rhetoric with extreme intimacy of tone, is profound. From Swinburne and Hopkins onwards, it has been a commonplace among critics to compare the young Keats with the young Shakespeare, and it is probably most specifically Keats's odes and Shakespeare's sonnets that the critics have in mind. The tribute of formal imitation which Arnold paid Keats in 'Thyrsis' and 'The Scholar Gypsy' is again probably a finer criticism, in a high sense of the word criticism, than his early denigration of Keats in his letters to Clough or even his later generous praise of Keats in his introduction to the Keats selections in Ward's *English Poets.*

I have not, of course, included 'Thyrsis' and 'The Scholar Gypsy' in this volume, any more than I have included any of the numerous passages in Tennyson which remind us of the odes in their pictorial quality, in their rich phrasing, in their autumnal plangency of mood. Poetry is the best criticism of poetry, but people who buy a volume of this sort are expecting to buy a selection of prose commentaries. What should be remembered is that the pervading influence of Keats in the Victorian age is to be found more in how good other poets found him to steal from than in prose commentaries. As Browning wrote:

> Who fished the murex up?
> What porridge had John Keats?

For Keats's sense, a classical and traditional sense, of transience Arnold substitutes in 'Thyrsis' and 'The Scholar Gypsy' the more local Victorian sense of the constant worry, hurry and push of historical change; for Keats's intuition of the eternal in nature, art and myth Arnold substitutes the idea of a temporary escape from Victorian public worries to the placid meadows round Oxford. 'Thyrsis' and 'The Scholar Gypsy' are beautiful poems, but, set against the odes, they seem diluted, local, minor. The exercise in imitation may have given Arnold his first awareness of Keats's real greatness, his permanent and classical quality.

II

To Keats's early reviewers, and to early commentators on him, the odes did not stand out as the crown of his work, as they do for us, though 'Nightingale' was popular and often quoted or anthologised. The very weaknesses of 'Nightingale', touches of plaintiveness and self-pity, lines like

> Here, where men sit and hear each other groan,

gave currency to the legend, propagated maliciously by Byron in *Don Juan* and in good faith by Shelley in *Adonais*, of Keats as a weak, womanly creature whose heart and health had been broken by Croker's savage review of *Endymion, A Poetic Romance* (1818) in the *Quarterly Review* and by Lockhart's much more personal and poisonous attack, an expression of Tory class-hatred, on 'Johnny Keats' and the Cockney School of Poetry in *Blackwood's*. In fact, Keats was as conscious of the weaknesses of *Endymion* as Croker himself (and, however deplorable his tone Croker's analysis of the faults of this narrative poem without thrust or design is a basically sound one), and, so far was he from being heart-broken that the year following these articles was the year of Keats's greatest poetic creation. His weak first volume, *Poems* (1817), which in fact had been treated by the reviewers more kindly than it deserved, and *Endymion* together would have left him, if he had died in 1818, with the reputation only of a minor poet, with some talent, largely misused. It was after the unfavourable reviews of *Endymion* that he gathered his forces together to produce, in the 1820 volume, one of the greatest single volumes of poetry of modern times. Unfortunately, about a fortnight before the appearance of the 1820 volume, Keats had had a haemorrhage which announced to him all too clearly, with his accurate medical knowledge, the fatal nature of his illness. The very favourable reviews which the new volume received could no more cheer him now than the attacks on *Endymion* and himself had been able to daunt him two years earlier. With his health, with his hopes of marrying Fanny Brawne, his confidence in his genius collapsed also. He died on 23 February 1821, eight months after the appearance of the volume that has given him immortal glory, instructing his friend Severn to put no name on his Roman tombstone, but only the phrase: 'Here lies one whose name was writ in water.'

The pathetic circumstances of Keats's death aroused sympathy, but, with Shelley's *Adonais,* helped to create a picture of Keats as an over-sensitive weakling, a picture which Arnold, Hopkins and Swinburne were still having to combat forty years later. The Victorian age was also on the whole a more snobbish period than the Romantic age, and the feeling carrying over from *Blackwood's* attacks that there was something mawkish and vulgar and effeminately self-indulgent in Keats's character, that he was no gentleman, hampered his Victorian public reputation; even Arnold and Swinburne are embarrassed by the Fanny Brawne letters; and the main service of Lord Houghton's biography of 1848 was its almost comic insistence that Keats was at least *almost* a gentleman – he was almost sent to Harrow, Houghton said, he knew some respectable and distinguished people, he was born 'in the upper rank of the middle-class' (Houghton, of course, was thinking of the class *below* his own class, that of the landed gentry and nobility, where when we today use the term 'middle class' we more often mean 'upper class', or a class which the writer, however respectable, does not quite think of himself as belonging to).

This Victorian snobbery fortunately did not affect poets. We have noticed Keats's direct influence on

Tennyson and on Arnold, though the young Arnold was in principle an anti-Keatsian. The whole pre-Raphaelite movement might be thought of as springing out of 'La Belle Dame Sans Merci' and 'The Eve of St Agnes'. Hopkins, so different in temperament from Keats, and disapproving of his sensuality, is yet sensual or sensuous in a Keatsian way himself; the bitter or sweet sloe bursting in the mouth and filling the whole being in 'The Wreck of the *Deutschland*' is sensuous in the same manner as the 'draught of vintage' at the beginning of 'Nightingale'. Hopkins defends Keats's 'manliness' in a letter to Canon Dixon (an obsession with 'manliness' was not confined to muscular Christians such as Charles Kingsley and Tom Hughes), observing truly that it is not only women who are sensual. In this letter, like Swinburne, he picks out the odes for special praise and dwells on Keats's Shakespearean quality.

III

Victorian criticism of poetry tended to be either general and prescriptive, or cursory and panoramic. It was not until the 1870s and 1880s that the scholarly study of fairly recent literature began to become a profession, and that publishers began to commission book-length studies of nineteenth-century poets. The first book-length study of Keats appeared in 1880. Its author, Mrs F. M. Owen, the wife of a clergyman-schoolmaster who had been an Oxford don, is strongly influenced in style and attitudes by Walter Pater. She dwells almost gloatingly on 'that languor and failure of the springs of life' which she finds in 'Nightingale', on the sense in 'Nightingale' and 'Indolence' both of 'the failure of vitality, the beginning of the end, the appealing beauty of the flower which is about to fall'. This is a *fin-de-siècle,* almost an *Art nouveau* Keats. Mrs Owen, however, responds not only to the sense of 'the sadness of all joy' in 'Melancholy' but to the health and serenity of 'To Autumn'. She is the first critic to use

Keats's letters to throw detailed light on the odes, and she quotes:

> I never liked the stubble fields so much as now; ay, better than the chilly green of spring. Somehow a stubble plain looks warm in the way some pictures look warm. They struck me so much in my Sunday's walk that I composed upon it.

(Compare the exact transcription from the Hyder Rollins edition of Keats's letters in the body of the text. The tendency of nineteenth-century printers and publishers to conventionalise an author's punctuation creates some of the textual problems about 'Urn'.) She ranks 'Urn' highest among the odes, for its 'wide-ranging thought ... high conception ... and repressed feeling'. The same year, 1880, saw the publication of Arnold's fine tribute to Keats in his note on him in Ward's *English Poets*. As a young man, Arnold had considered Keats as a very bad influence, a poet of beautiful scattered images without leading ideas or a unifying sense of structure. In 1880 he sees that there is 'flint and iron' in Keats and quotes approvingly the famous (and later much criticised) conclusion of 'Urn'. Arnold sees 'Beauty is truth, truth beauty' as certainly not *all* we need to know, but as a partial truth we *must* know. He now sees that Keats is anything but a poet without leading ideas:

> It is no small thing to have so loved the principle of beauty as to perceive the necessary relation of beauty with truth, and of both with joy ...

The 1880s also saw Swinburne's fine tribute to Keats, first printed in the *Encyclopaedia Britannica*, and later collected in the volume *Miscellanies*. Swinburne's shrill tone of voice can disguise from modern readers what a good critic he is; apart from an over-estimation of the plays, his relative placing of Keats's various poems is almost exactly that of the best modern criticism.

The most distinguished, however, of the early appreciators of Keats was the poet Robert Bridges. In 1896 he printed, privately, a small edition of *A Critical Introduction to the Poems of John Keats*. Bridges's chapter on the odes in this little book is, however wrong-headed one may feel some of it to be, the one magisterial treatment of these poems: rather similarly, his often wrong-headed and unfair introduction to the first edition (1918) of his friend Hopkins's poems remains a more lively and provocative piece of English critical prose than the subsequent more enthusiastic or more scholarly introductions of Charles Williams and W. H. Gardner. He has the courage of assertive positive judgement. He rates 'Urn' lower than any other critic, finding in it merely the repetitive illustration of a true but trite idea. He rates 'Psyche', which Professor Kenneth Allott has well described as 'the Cinderella of the great Odes', higher than any other critic except T. S. Eliot, who thought it the finest of them all. He ranked 'Autumn' first. Next came 'Nightingale' for its 'splendour', 'richness' and 'variety'. Next came 'Melancholy' for what we would today call its emotional sincerity (it is interesting that Bridges, unlike that much less loyal servant of moral and social convention than himself, William Empson, is not morally perturbed by 'Melancholy', though he does note in passing, in another section of his book, that to present a loved one's 'rich anger' as an object, like a flower, of detached aesthetic appreciation is odd). 'Psyche' came after 'Melancholy', and 'Urn' disputed with 'Indolence' the last place. 'Maia' was praised as a splendid fragment.

IV

These late Victorian critics had isolated the odes as a group of poems deserving special admiration and attention, and had drawn attention to the problem of the order of excellence of the poems within the group, and by their very disagreements with each other had suggested that there might be problems about the meanings, tones and structures of the odes. The treatment of the odes by twentieth-century critics can be thought of under three main headings: a scholarly approach to the text and the history of its composition, in which the two main figures are H. W. Garrod and M. R. Ridley; long critical essays or chapters on the odes as a group or on individual odes and their problems, in which modern methods of close reading or structural analysis are employed; and biographical approaches to the odes, to the conditions of their composition, using Keats's letters and other contemporary material. Summarily, one can distinguish between the scholarly or textual, the analytic and the biographical approach.

The present selection of essays is mainly though not solely concerned with the second of these three categories, with close readings of the odes. The odes lend themselves more easily than other poems of Keats's to the methods of what in America is called 'the New Criticism'. They are at once short enough to be apprehended as wholes in a single reading and long enough, and complex and difficult enough in their modulation, to reward detailed analysis. Of Keats's longer narrative poems, only 'The Eve of St Agnes' is a completely successful work of art; in the others, including the two versions of 'Hyperion', we admire the effort but we do not enjoy the whole. In poems shorter than the odes, Keats is notoriously uneven. He was not a master of the lyrical short poem in the sense, say, that Blake was. Of his shorter and slighter poems, only 'In a drear-nighted December' haunts the ear, only 'La Belle Dame Sans Merci' haunts the imagination. Among many bad, he wrote some good sonnets, but nobody would rank him as a writer of sonnets with Shakespeare, Milton or Wordsworth. Much of his more ambitious writing, the deplorable 'Cap and Bells', 'King Otho', perhaps *Endymion* itself, strikes a modern reader as not only uneven in execution but wrong in its basic conception. Among so many pages in which genius has mistaken its object, or is expending itself on trifles, the odes stand out in Keats's work by their assurance and originality. They are essentially a new and modern kind of poem.

The basic theme of the odes, the tension between our painful sense of transience and our intuitions of the eternal, the relationship, in a more abstract sense, between the pain of life and the delight of poetry, the relationship, in a more abstract sense still, between life, art and death is a central theme of modern poetry. Yeats's 'Sailing to Byzantium' and 'Byzantium', for instance, can be read as modern variations on the themes of Keats's odes and, though they are great poems, they are not greater than the odes. The odes are also modern in that they are symbolic poems; they show, rather than say. They are modern in finding 'objective correlatives', artistically distanced, for intimate and painful states of personal feeling. We get away in them from the too 'personal touch', that faintly cloying note, which flaws so much of Keats's other work; the note which Byron described so brutally but not wholly inaccurately as that of 'self-soliciting', that of self-induced erotic excitement: the note which *Blackwood's* thought of as the mawkishness of 'Johnny Keats'. The elimination of the 'personal touch', though not of the properly personal tone, the achievement without strain (like the strain of *Hyperion*) of self-transcendence, is at once the triumph and in a sense the argument, or plot, of the odes. Keats finds himself, and finds us, as a poet, in his willingness at last completely to lose himself.

I have made a distinction between three kinds of criticism; I should make a subsidiary distinction between two kinds of modern critic represented in this volume, the English and the North American. For the North American critics the odes are most aptly approached as symbolic structures, symbolic presentations and resolutions of tense and paradoxical inner states. They approach a poem almost in the frame of mind of the engineer, looking for the pushes and pulls that hold it together, the conquered elements of inertia or friction, the dynamic that makes it work. Kenneth Burke and Cleanth Brooks typify this approach at its most extreme. English critics of the odes have on the whole clung to the Arnoldian tradition of seeing poetry as a 'criticism of life'. They have been concerned with the human or moral meaning of the odes, and this is true not only of Middleton Murry or F. R. Leavis (whom I omit for reasons of space), very consciously moralistic critics, but true of William Empson, whose close linguistic analysis of the paradoxes of 'Melancholy' is essentially a criticism of something that seems to him extreme and over-strained in romantic attitudes. Very broadly, in Keats's own terms, the American critics are more concerned with the 'beauty' of the odes, the English with their 'truth'.

This brings us to the one great textual and interpretative crux in the odes, that concerned with the last two lines of the last stanza of 'Urn'. In the Oxford edition, Garrod prints the last part of this stanza thus:

> Cold Pastoral!
> When old age shall this generation waste,
> Thou shalt remain, in midst of other woe
> Than ours, a friend to man, to whom thou say'st,
> Beauty is truth, truth beauty, – that is all
> Ye know on earth, and all ye need to know.

The ode was twice printed in Keats's lifetime, first early in 1820, in *Annals of the Fine Arts*, where the last two lines read:

> Beauty is Truth, Truth Beauty. – That is all
> Ye know on Earth, and all ye need to know.

In the 1820 volume the penultimate line is:

> 'Beauty is truth, truth beauty', that is all . . .

We have no autograph but there are four transcripts,

by George Keats, Charles Wentworth Dilke, Charles Armitage Brown and Richard Woodhouse. They read, respectively:

> Beauty is truth, – Truth Beauty, – that is all . . .
>
> Beauty is truth, – truth beauty, – that is all . . .
>
> Beauty is Truth, – Truth Beauty, – that is all . . .
>
> Beauty is Truth, – Truth beauty, – That is all . . .

It should be noticed that Dilke is consistent in his use of lower-case initials and Brown in his use of capitals for the words *truth* and *beauty* within the interior of the line. The other two are inconsistent. Where the transcripts differ importantly from the early printings is in the second dash in the second last line, and the lack of the quotation marks which in the 1820 volume and the full stop which in *Annals* tend to make us take 'Beauty is truth, truth beauty' as the end of the urn's statement, and the last line and a half of the poem as a statement directly by Keats. It might be thought, however, that Woodhouse's capital *t* for 'That' in fact makes the last line and a half a separate statement and suggests that his preceding comma should be a full stop. Gerald Bullett, the editor of the Everyman edition, who takes it that the urn is speaking to the end, amends the punctuation thus:

> 'Beauty is truth, truth beauty, – that is all
> Ye know on earth, and all ye need to know.'

If we take the last line and a half as spoken by Keats (which, basing myself more on the two early printings than on the transcripts. I would like to do) there are two alternatives. Either Keats is, as he has been doing throughout the ode, addressing the figures on the urn or he is, abruptly, confusingly and with a breach of decorum, addressing his readers for the first time in the ode. If he is addressing the figures on the urn there is no real puzzle; the truth and beauty, the existence and value, of figures in a work of art *are* identical. The whole poem has been saying that these figures are caught in a moment of stasis, free from human pain and struggle. The implication is that though art's message of some sort of ultimate identity of the true and the beautiful, the real and the ideal, makes art a 'friend to man', still *we*, 'this generation', as opposed to *ye*, the figures on the urn, need to know a great deal more than this, though we need to know this too. That was essentially how Matthew Arnold took it.

But if either the urn is addressing mankind to the end of the stanza or Keats is suddenly reinforcing the urn's message on his own behalf, then with Quiller-Couch, T. S. Eliot and many others we cannot help feeling that 'Beauty is truth, truth beauty' is inadequate as a summary of *all* that we need in the way of saving wisdom. There is evidence that Keats underpunctuated, used capitals erratically and, though a very careful verbal reviser, may have been willing to leave matters of punctuation to his printers. The transcripts, in spite of their discrepancies, are probably nearer his own manuscript or manuscripts than either of the early printings; and George Keats's, Dilke's and Brown's transcripts, though not so certainly Woodhouse's, on the whole, with their extra dash, which Woodhouse also has, are in favour of such an emendation of the original printings as Bullett's. I think Garrod, though leaning on Woodhouse's transcript, meant to leave the options open.

This difficult textual problem has, however, been less discussed than the question of what exactly either Keats or the Urn can have *meant* by 'Beauty is truth, truth beauty'. Keats's famous letter to Bailey, of which the most relevant portion is included in this compilation, makes it clear what some of the possible ranges of meaning could be. Keats was a man of swift intuitive perceptions and the thought of arriving at truth by a long laborious process of abstract reasoning repelled him. He was also a man with a firm, though not orthodoxly Christian, belief in an afterlife. He thought of heaven as a repetition, with ever greater understanding, of the moments of beauty we have known on earth, just as he thought our highest experience on earth is the intense imaginative re-living of such moments. Such moments are not meaningless, are not mere reverie or fantasy, but give us a foretaste of what life in heaven will be like, or sudden intense glimpses of the ultimate harmony of things. There is some evidence that he thought of 'truth' not as the abstract correspondence of proposition and fact but as a living pattern of identity in actual things, something like Hopkins's 'inscape', which imagination or intuition grasps in a way that abstract reasoning or 'cold philosophy' (what we would now call science) never can.

There must be something wrong with the last stanza, or it would not have bothered so many critics so much, but the flaw is in the machinery of the syntax – had Keats, in fact, quite made up his *own* mind whether it was he or the urn that was speaking in the last line and a half? – rather than any inconsistency in Keats's thought. One could complain, at the most, that without knowledge of Keats's letter to Bailey there is a danger of taking 'Beauty is truth, truth beauty' as an abstract philosophical statement (a truism to Platonists, but very worrying to Aristotelians) rather than as a personal affirmation, based on Keats's experience as a poet and his very personal religious vision.

V

I have been faced with a number of problems in making this selection. 'Urn' and 'Nightingale' have been by far the most popular of the odes, though many critics have recognised the special quality, the serene perfection, the impersonal chastity, of 'To Autumn'. There is not very much on 'Psyche', which Bridges ranked high and T. S. Eliot highest among the odes, but which Professor Allott calls the Cinderella among them. 'Melancholy', though generally recognised as a rich and beautiful poem, has also been comparatively neglected, and 'Indolence' fairly generally dismissed as a failure. I have tried to keep a fair balance between the different odes. I thought also that I should try to keep a balance between English and American critics, but the general editor rightly persuaded me that the important thing was to choose good essays, wherever or by whomever they had been written. I would like specially to thank the American poet and critic, the author of an excellent study of Elizabeth Bishop, Anne Stevenson, for her help. She had many articles photostated for me in Cambridge, and her own critical comments on them, and on the odes, were most helpful. Her name really ought to be along with mine on the title-page as co-editor of this book.

Finally, it has been fascinating in making this selection to watch the great odes of Keats being gradually singled out as a group, being given a preferential status in Keats's *œuvre*, receiving a scholarly examination that defines their originality of form, being rooted by biographers in Keats's life and place and time, and at last, for their closest modern readers, transcending that life and place and time, as the 'Urn' and the 'Nightingale' transcended them, and becoming part of the living fabric of whatever it is one means by 'modern poetry'. I have been given a new sense of criticism as a continuous and co-operative activity, to which small as well as great men can contribute, if they make the proper effort, at the right point in time.

G. S. Fraser

PART ONE

The Poet on the Odes

EXTRACTS FROM KEATS'S LETTERS

Ode to May

With respect to the affections and Poetry you must know by a sympathy my thoughts that way; and I dare say these few lines will be but a ratification: I wrote them on May-day – and intend to finish the ode all in good time. –

Mother of Hermes! and still youthful Maia!
    May I sing to thee
As thou wast hymned on the shores of Baiae?
    Or may I woo thee
In earlier Sicilian? or thy smiles
Seek as they once were sought, in Grecian isles,
By Bards who died content on pleasant sward,
Leaving great verse unto a little clan?
O give me their old vigour, and unheard
Save of the quiet Primrose, and the span//
Of Heaven, and few ears//rounded by thee,
My song should die away// content as <this> theirs//
Rich in the simple worship of a day. –//

(to J. H. Reynolds, 3 May 1818)

Ode to Psyche

The following Poem – the last I have written and the first and the only one with which I have taken even moderate pains – I have for the most part dash'd of (*sic*) my lines in a hurry – This I have done leisurely – I think it reads the more richly for it and will I hope encourage me to write other thing[s] in even a more peacable and healthy spirit. You must recollect that Psyche was not embodied as a goddess before the time of Apulieus (*sic*) the Platonist who lived afteir (*sic*) the Agustan age (*sic*), and consequently the Goddess was never worshipped or sacrificed to with any of the ancient fervour – and perhaps never thought of in the old religion – I am more orthodox that (*sic*) to let a hethen (*sic*) Goddess be so neglected –

[Draft of 'Ode to Psyche' follows]

(to George and Georgiana Keats, April 1819)

Ode to a Nightingale

... O there is nothing like fine weather, and health, and Books, and a fine country, and a contented Mind, and Diligent-habit of reading and thinking, and an amulet against the ennui – and please heaven, a little claret-wine cool out of a cellar a mile deep – with a few or a good many ratafia cakes – rocky basin to bathe in, a strawberry bed to say your prayers to Flora in....

[Compare stanza two of the 'Ode to a Nightingale']

(to Fanny Keats, 1 May 1819)

George is busy this morning in making copies of my verse – He is now making one of an Ode to the nightingale, which is like reading an account of the back (*sic*) hole of Calcutta on an ice bergh (*sic*).

(to Georgiana Keats, 15 January 1820)

Ode on a Grecian Urn

...But I am running my head into a Subject which I am certain I could not do justice to under five years s[t]udy and 3 vols octavo – and moreover long to be talking about the Imagination – ... O I wish I was as certain of the end of all your troubles as that of your momentary start about the authenticity of the Imagination. I am certain of nothing but the holiness of the Heart's affections and the truth of Imagination – What the imagination seizes as Beauty must be truth – whether it existed before or not – for I have the same Idea of all our Passions as of Love they are all in their sublime, creative of essential Beauty – In a Word, you may know my favorite Speculation by my first book and the little song I sent in my last – which is a representation from the fancy of the probable mode of operating in these matters – The Imagination may be compared to Adam's dream – he awoke and found it truth. I am the more zealous in this affair, because I have never yet been able to perceive how any thing can be known for truth by consequitive (*sic*) reasoning – and yet it must be – Can it be that even the greatest Philosopher ever <when> arrived at his goal without putting aside numerous objections – However it may be, O for a Life of Sensations rather than of Thoughts! It is 'a Vision in the form of Youth' a Shadow of reality to come – and this consideration has further conv[i]nced me for it has come as auxiliary to another favorite Speculation of mine, that we shall enjoy ourselves here after by having what we call happiness on Earth repeated in a finer tone and so repeated – And yet such a fate can only befall those who delight in sensation rather than hunger as you do after Truth – Adam's dream will do here and seems to be a conviction that Imagination and its empyreal reflection is the same as human Life and its spiritual repetition. But as I was saying – the simple imaginative Mind may have its rewards in the repeti[ti]on of its own silent Working coming continually on the spirit with a fine suddenness – to compare great things with small – have you never by being surprised with an old Melody – in a delicious place – by a delicious voice, fe[l]t over again your very speculations and surmises at the time it first operated on your soul – do you not remember forming to yourself the singer's face more beautiful that (*sic*) it was possible and yet with the elevation of the Moment you do not think so high – that the prototype must be here after – that delicious face you will see – What a time! I am continually running away from the subject – sure this cannot be exactly the case with a complex Mind – one that is imaginative and at the same time careful of its fruits – who would exist partly on sensation partly on thought – to whom it is necessary that years should bring the philosophic Mind

– such an one I consider your's and therefore it is necessary to your eternal Happiness that you not only drink <have> this old Wine of Heaven which I shall call the redigestion of our most ethereal Musings on Earth; but also increase in knowledge and know all things ...

(to Benjamin Bailey, 22 November 1817)

The sacrifice goes on; the pontif knife
Gleams in the sun, the milk-white heifer lows,
The pipes go shrilly, the libation flows....
For in the world
We jostle – but my flag is not unfurled
On the Admiral staff – and to philosophize
I dare not yet! – Oh never will the prize,
High reason, and the lore of good and ill
Be my award. Things cannot to the will
Be settled, but they tease us out of thought.
Or is it that Imagination brought
Beyond its proper bound, yet still confined, –
Lost in a sort of Purgatory blind,
Cannot refer to any standard law
Of either earth or heaven? – It is a flaw
In happiness to see beyond our bourn –
It forces us in Summer skies to mourn:
It spoils the singing of the Nightingale.

(verse letter to J. H. Reynolds, 23 March 1818)

Ode to Autumn

How beautiful the season is now – How fine the air. A temperate sharpness about it. Really, without joking, chaste weather – Dian skies – I never lik'd stubble fields so much as now – Aye better than the chilly green of the spring. Somehow a stubble plain looks warm – in the same way that some pictures look warm – this struck me so much in my sunday's walk that I composed upon it.

(to J. H. Reynolds, 21 September 1819)

Ode on Indolence

... This morning I am in a sort of temper indolent and supremely careless: I long after a stanza or two of Thompson's Castle of indolence – My passions are all asleep from my having slumbered till nearly eleven and weakened the animal fibre all over me to a delightful sensation about three degrees on this side of faintness – if I had teeth of pearl and the breath of lillies I should call it langour (*sic*) but as I am† I must call it Laziness – In this state of effeminacy the fibres of the brain are relaxed in common with the rest of the body, and to such a happy degree that pleasure has no show of enticement and pain no unbearable frown. Neither Poetry, nor Ambition, nor Love have any alertness of countenance as they pass by me: they seem rather like three figures on a greek vase – a Man and two women – whom no one but myself could distinguish in their disguisement. This is the only happiness; and is a rare instance of advantage in the body overpowering the Mind.

† especially as I have a black eye

(to the George Keatses, 19 March 1819)

I have been very idle lately, very averse to writing; both from the overpowering idea of our dead poets and from abatement of my love of fame. I hope I am a little more of a Philosopher than I was, consequently a little less of a versifying Pet-Lamb. I have put no more in Print or you should have had it. You will judge of my 1819 temper when I tell you that the thing I have most enjoyed this year has been writing an ode to Indolence.

(to Sarah Jeffrey, 9 June 1819)

(from *The Letters of John Keats,* edited by Hyder E. Rollins, 2 vols, Cambridge, Mass., 1958)

PART TWO

Earlier Comments, 1848–95

RICHARD MONCKTON MILNES: Keats's Methods of Composition

... Shorter poems were scrawled, as they happened to suggest themselves, on the first scrap of paper at hand, which was afterwards used as a mark for a book, or thrown anywhere aside. It seemed as if, when his imagination was once relieved, by writing down its effusions, he cared so little about them that it required a friend at hand to prevent them from being utterly lost. The admirable 'Ode to a Nightingale' was suggested by the continual song of the bird that, in the spring of 1819, had built her nest close to the house, and which often threw Keats into a sort of trance of tranquil pleasure. One morning he took his chair from the breakfast-table, placed it on the grass-plot under a plum-tree, and sat there for two or three hours with some scraps of paper in his hands. Shortly afterwards Mr Brown saw him thrusting them away, as waste paper, behind some books, and had considerable difficulty in putting together and arranging the stanzas of the Ode. Other poems as literally 'fugitive' were rescued in much the same way – for he permitted Mr Brown to copy whatever he could pick up, and sometimes assisted him.

The odes 'To a Nightingale' and 'On a Grecian Urn' were first published in a periodical entitled the *Annals of Fine Arts*. Soon after he had composed them, he repeated, or rather chanted, them to Mr Haydon, in the sort of recitative that so well suited his deep grave voice, as they strolled together through Kilburn meadows, leaving an indelible impression on the mind of his surviving friend.

A singular instance of Keats's delicate perception occurred in the composition of the 'Ode on Melancholy'. In the original manuscript, he had intended to represent the vulgar connection of Melancholy with gloom and horror, in contrast with the emotion that incites to,

> glut thy sorrow on a morning rose,
> Or on the rainbow of the salt sand-wave,
> Or on the wealth of globed peonies;

and which essentially

> dwells with Beauty – Beauty that must die,
> And Joy, whose hand is ever at his lips
> Bidding adieu.

The first stanza, therefore, was the following: as grim a picture as Blake or Fuseli could have dreamed and painted:

> Though you should build a bark of dead men's bones,
> And rear a phantom gibbet for a mast,
> Stitch shrouds together for a sail, with groans
> To fill it out, blood-stained and aghast;
> Although your rudder be a dragon's tail
> Long severed, yet still hard with agony,
> Your cordage large uprootings from the skull
> Of bald Medusa, certes you would fail
> To find the Melancholy – whether she
> Dreameth in any isle of Lethe dull.

But no sooner was this written than the poet became conscious that the coarseness of the contrast would destroy the general effect of luxurious tenderness which it was the object of the poem to produce, and he confined the gross notion of Melancholy to less violent images, and let the ode at once begin,

> No, no, go not to Lethe, neither twist
> Wolf's-bane, tight-rooted, for its poisonous wine;
> Nor suffer thy pale forehead to be kiss'd
> By nightshade, ruby grape of Proserpine ...

(from *Life, Letters and Literary Remains of John Keats*, 1848)

MRS F. M. OWEN: 'A quickly generated sympathy'

The work of most poets might be divided into that

which is the result of purpose and that which is the result of circumstance. The result of purpose is generally the outcome of the poet's life of inner thought, that which he has individually won for himself out of all the influences of his time, and this is his maturest work, his most deliberate expression. Such was Shelley's 'Prometheus', Wordsworth's 'Excursion', and such would also have been the 'Hyperion' of Keats.

But the poetry whose inspiration comes suddenly from a quickly generated sympathy with passing circumstance has a value of its own exceeding in some ways that of more premeditated work, for it pictures to us more vividly the human life of the writer. The actual life of Keats (as moved or touched by human circumstance), which is revealed in the Odes and Sonnets, makes clearer to us the underlying human truths of 'Endymion' and 'Hyperion'. Such a poem as the 'Ode to a Nightingale' (written on scraps of paper and thrust away as waste behind some books) is a spontaneous expression of the life the poet was then living. The nightingale sang in the plum-tree at Wentworth Place, and Keats sat and listened to it, and wrote one of the saddest and sweetest poems in our language. It was written in the same year and nearly at the same time as 'Lamia', when the shadow of his approaching doom seemed to be stealing over him, when his brother Tom, whom he had loved so well, had lately died, when he was waking to consciousness of the love that was his fate. There is noticeable all through the poem that languor and failure of the springs of life which marks the first approach of death, however distant the event may be, and that remarkably quickened sympathy with all natural life which is so often to be seen in those who are doomed to die. It was this sympathy which made Keats write a few months later, 'How astonishingly does the chance of leaving the world impress a sense of its natural beauties upon us! The simple flowers of our spring are what I want to see again.'[1]

It was therefore no mere poetic wish, but the expression of a real sadness, which prompted the longing 'to fade away into the forest dim' with the nightingale.

Fade far away, dissolve, and quite forget
What thou among the leaves hast never known,
The weariness, the fever, and the fret,
Here, where men sit and hear each other groan:
Where palsy shakes a few sad last grey hairs,
Where youth grows pale, and spectre-thin, and dies;
Where but to think is to be full of sorrow
And leaden-eyed despairs;
Where beauty cannot keep her lustrous eyes,
Or new love pine at them beyond to-morrow.

We can imagine, too, how his thoughts were haunted by the suffering of his brother's last weeks, when he wrote of being 'half in love with *easeful* death'; and how true it is in that passionately loving nature, which loved even its brothers with more than the love of women, that thinking of Tom in his new-made grave, and of George far away in America, John Keats should write from his heart,

Forlorn! the very word is like a bell,
To toll me back from thee to my sole self.

The whole of this magical ode seems to make life vocal for us as we read it, but it also brings us very close to the wearied young heart that was nearing death.

A few months later it was the quiet Sunday walk through the stubble fields near Winchester which won for us the 'Ode to Autumn', a walk of which Keats writes: 'I never liked stubble fields as much as now; ay, better than the chilly green of spring. Somehow a stubble plain looks warm in the way some pictures look warm. This struck me so much in my Sunday's walk that I composed upon it.' And who is there that has not realised the charm of that English landscape described in the

Season of mists and mellow fruitfulness,

and does not feel the autumnal glory which had touched the poet when he wrote:—

Where are the songs of Spring? Ay, where are they?
  Think not of them, thou hast thy music too,
While barred clouds bloom the soft-dying day,
  And touch the stubble-plains with rosy hue.

Of the 'Ode to Psyche' Keats says in a letter written to his brother in America, in March 1819: 'The following poem, the last I have written, is the first and only one with which I have taken even moderate pains. I have for the most part dashed off my lines in a hurry: this one I have done leisurely. I think it reads the more richly for it, and it will, I hope, encourage me to write other things in even a more peaceable and healthy spirit. You must recollect that Psyche was not embodied as a goddess before the time of Apuleius the Platonist, who lived after the Augustan age, and consequently the goddess was never worshipped or sacrificed to with any of the ancient fervour, and perhaps never thought of in the old religion. I am more orthodox than to let a heathen goddess be so neglected.'

This note explains the careful work which resulted in the condensation of beauty in this Ode, the wonderful music of its progress, and the exquisite spirituality of its thoughts. It is a link between 'Hyperion' and the other poems, for Psyche is

> ... latest born and loveliest vision far
> Of all Olympus' faded hierarchy!

though she has come to the world too late for temple, shrine, or 'pale-mouth'd prophet'.

O brightest! though too late for antique vows,
  Too, too late for the fond believing lyre,
When holy were the haunted forest boughs,
  Holy the air, the water, and the fire.

Again, we feel the wondrous power of realising the past and uniting it with the present and the future, which was one of the peculiar inspirations of the genius of Keats. This link with the 'faint Olympians' has in it the very principle of continuity, the recognition of the growing soul of the ages. For that prophetic gaze, drawing from the past the undying principle of beauty, which it saw also in a distant future, found a fitness in the absence of Psyche from the deities of long ago. It is 'the latest born, the loveliest vision far'; it comes into the world unrecognised and as yet unworshipped save by one here and there, 'who sees and sings by his own eyes inspired'. But such an one will be its priest, and in 'some untrodden region of the mind' its sanctuary shall be made,

Where branchèd thoughts, new-grown with pleasant pain,
Instead of pines shall murmur in the wind.

The 'Ode on Melancholy' seems to have been partly influenced by the verses at the commencement of Burton's 'Anatomy of Melancholy', which suggest that fulfilled joy is melancholy, and that the other side of every pleasure is pain. But the thought of Keats goes beyond this, he sees the sadness of all joy, and that it is not the acknowledged grief of our lives which is the secret of true melancholy. but that our gladness should be what it is. It is not the wolf's-bane, the night-shade, the yew berries, the death-moth, that are the saddest emblems; it is 'the morning rose', 'the rainbow of the salt sand-wave', 'the wealth of globed peonies', 'the peerless eyes' of her that is loved. The most sorrowful reality of melancholy is that

She dwells with Beauty – Beauty that must die,
And Joy whose hand is ever at his lips,
Bidding adieu.

A curious change was made in the original, and Lord Houghton quotes an opening verse of it which was suppressed as being disproportionately horrible to the rest. It is one of the grimmest word-pictures Keats ever drew.

Though you should build a bark of dead men's bones,
  And rear a phantom gibbet for a mast,
Stitch shrouds together for a sail, with groans
  To fill it out, blood-stainèd and aghast;
Although your rudder be a dragon's tail
  Long sever'd, yet still hard with agony,
Your cordage large uprootings from the skull
  Of bald Medusa, certes you would fail
To find the melancholy – whether she
  Dreameth in any isle of Lethe dull.

In the 'Ode on Indolence', the passing and repassing of the shadowy figures of Love, Ambition, and Poetry, and the weariness with which the poet looks at them and turns from them, brings to us the same feeling as the 'Ode to the Nightingale', the failure of vitality, the beginning of the end, the appealing beauty of the flower which is about to fall. It is a depth of suffering loneliness that no human comfort could reach or touch which speaks to us from the words,

> Farewell! I yet have visions for the night,
> And for the day faint visions there is store.

Very different is the Ode which commences,

> Bards of Passion and of Mirth,
> Ye have left your souls on earth!
> Have ye souls in heaven too,
> Double-lived in regions new?

It is in a short monotonous metre, but is full of fire and of human feeling, and its joyous hopefulness contrasts with the sadness in most of the other odes.

After imagining the joys on which the souls of poets have entered,

> Where the daisies are rose-scented,
> And the rose herself has got
> Perfume which on earth is not.
> Where the nightingale doth sing
> Not a senseless trancèd thing,
> But divine melodious truth;

it goes on to glory in the thought that in their works these same souls are still living on earth, and that those who are able to receive them are prepared by them for their further life of joy, so that they are double lived.

> Thus ye live on high, and then
> On the earth ye live again;
> And the souls ye left behind you
> Teach us, here, the way to find you,
> Where your other souls are joying,
> Never slumber'd, never cloying.
> Here your earth-born souls still speak
> To mortals, of their little week;
> Of their sorrows and delights,
> Of their passions and their spites,
> Of their glory and their shame,
> What doth strengthen and what maim.
> Thus ye teach us every day
> Wisdom, though fled far away.

The same idea is to be found in a less elevated form in the lines on the Mermaid Tavern.

But the wide-reaching thought, the high conception, and the repressed feeling of the 'Ode on a Grecian Urn' make it perhaps the crowning glory of the shorter poems. It is the inspiration of one of those hours when the quiet of the great past seems a more powerful influence than the action of the present or purposes of the future. It is not joyful, for its thought is too calm for joy, and it is not sorrowful, for its calm is too deep for sorrow. It has gathered from all time the abiding principle of Beauty, and sees in its undying power the true friend of man.

ODE ON A GRECIAN URN

> Thou still unravish'd bride of quietness
>   Thou foster-child of silence and slow time,

Sylvan historian, who canst thus express
  A flowery tale more sweetly than our rhyme;
What leaf-fringed legend haunts about thy shape
  Of deities or mortals, or of both
    In Tempe or the dales of Arcady?
What men or gods are these? what maidens loth?
  What mad pursuit, what struggle to escape?
    What pipes and timbrels? what wild ecstasy?

Heard melodies are sweet, but those unheard
  Are sweeter; therefore, ye soft pipes, play on;
Not to the sensual ear, but, more endear'd,
  Pipe to the spirit ditties of no tone;
Fair youth beneath the trees, thou canst not leave
  Thy song, nor ever can those trees be bare;
    Bold lover, never, never canst thou kiss,
Though winning near the goal – yet, do not grieve;
  She cannot fade, though thou hast not thy bliss,
    For ever wilt thou love, and she be fair!

Ah, happy happy boughs! that cannot shed
  Your leaves, nor ever bid the spring adieu;
And, happy melodist, unwearied,
  For ever piping songs for ever new;
More happy love! more happy, happy love!
  For ever warm and still to be enjoy'd,
    For ever panting, and for ever young;
All breathing human passion far above,
  That leaves a heart high sorrowful and cloy'd,
    A burning forehead and a parching tongue.

Who are these coming to the sacrifice?
  To what green altar, O mysterious priest,
Lead'st thou that heifer lowing at the skies,
  And all her silken flanks with garlands drest?
What little town by river or sea-shore,
  Or mountain-built with peaceful citadel,
    Is emptied of its folk this pious morn?
And, little town, thy streets for evermore
  Will silent be; and not a soul to tell
    Why thou art desolate, can e'er return.

O Attic shape! Fair attitude! with brede
Of marble men and maidens overwrought,
With forest branches and the trodden weed;
Thou silent form! dost tease us out of thought
As doth eternity: Cold Pastoral!
When old age shall this generation waste,
Thou shalt remain, in midst of other woe
Than ours, a friend to man, to whom thou say'st
'Beauty is truth, truth beauty' – that is all
Ye know on earth, and all ye need to know.

The Past is made alive in these words, its beauty has never died, and the very material in which the Attic shape is wrought is infused with life, the love of 'the happy melodist, unwearied',

For ever piping songs for ever new;

the sacrifice of the mysterious priest, 'the little town by river or sea-shore', from which the folk have come 'this pious morn', are real to us.

The 'Ode to the Nightingale' is full of a pathos and regret which are quite absent here, but the Grecian Urn represents a higher phase of thought. There is a touch of bitterness mingled with the poet's joy in the immortality of the nightingale's music.

Thou wast not born for death, immortal Bird!
No hungry generations tread thee down;
The voice I hear this passing night was heard
In ancient days by emperor and clown.

But there is no bitterness in the quieted spirit which has been so penetrated by the beauty of a bygone age that it can joy to know of this symbol of Greek calm.

When old age shall this generation waste,
Thou shalt remain, in midst of other woe
Than ours, a friend to man, to whom thou say'st,
'Beauty is truth, truth beauty' – that is all
Ye know on earth, and all ye need to know.

(from *John Keats: A Study,* 1880)

NOTE

1. Tennyson has touched on this sympathy of dying life in one of the most beautiful lines of the *May Queen*.

'I only wish to live till the snowdrops come again.'

A. C. SWINBURNE: 'The unequalled and unrivalled odes'

John Keats, born October 29, 1795, published his first volume of verse in 1817, his second in the following year, his third in 1820, and died of consumption at Rome, February 23, 1821, in the fourth month of his twenty-sixth year. In his first book there was little foretaste of anything greatly or even genuinely good; but between the marshy and sandy flats of sterile or futile verse there were undoubtedly some few purple patches of floral promise. The style was frequently detestable – a mixture of sham Spenserian and mock Wordsworthian, alternately florid and arid. His second book, *Endymion*, rises in its best passages to the highest level of Barnfield and of Lodge, the two previous poets with whom, had he published nothing more, he might properly have been classed; and this, among minor minstrels, is no unenviable place. His third book raised him at once to a foremost rank in the highest class of English poets. Never was any one of them but Shelley so little of a marvellous boy and so suddenly revealed as a marvellous man. Never has any poet suffered so much from the chaotic misarrangement of his poems in every collected edition.[1] The rawest and the rankest rubbish of his fitful spring is bound up in one sheaf with the ripest ears, flung into one basket with the richest fruits, of his sudden and splendid summer. The 'Ode to a Nightingale', one of the final masterpieces of human work in all time and for all ages, is immediately preceded in all editions now current by some of the most vulgar and fulsome doggrel ever whimpered by a vapid and effeminate rhymester in the sickly stage of whelphood....

No little injustice has been done to Keats by such devotees as fix their mind's eye only on the more salient and distinctive notes of a genius which in fact was very much more various and tentative, less limited and peculiar, than would be inferred from an exclusive study of his more specially characteristic work. But within the limits of that work must we look of course for the genuine credentials of his fame; and highest among them we must rate his unequalled and unrivalled odes. Of these perhaps the two nearest to absolute perfection, to the triumphant achievement and accomplishment of the very utmost beauty possible to human words, may be that to Autumn and that on a Grecian Urn; the most radiant, fervent, and musical is that to a Nightingale; the most pictorial and perhaps the tenderest in its ardour of passionate fancy is that to Psyche; the subtlest in sweetness of thought and feeling is that on Melancholy. Greater lyrical poetry the world may have seen than any that is in these; lovelier it surely has never seen, nor ever can it possibly see. From the divine fragment of an unfinished ode to Maia we can but guess that if completed it would have been worthy of a place beside the highest. His remaining lyrics have many beauties about them, but none perhaps can be called thoroughly beautiful. He has certainly left us one perfect sonnet of the first rank; and as certainly he has left us but one.

(from *Miscellanies*, 1886; reprinted from *Encyclopaedia Britannica*, 1882)

NOTE

1. This negligence has been remedied since the first appearance of this notice, and a more rational arrangement has been adopted.

G. M. HOPKINS: 'He had found the right way in his Odes'

During the summer examinations one of my colleagues brought in one day a *St James's Gazette*[1] with a piece of criticism he said it was a rare pleasure to read. It proved to be a review by you of Colvin's book on Keats. Still, enlightening as the review was, I did not think it really just. You classed Keats with the feminine geniuses among men and you would have it that he was not the likest but rather the unlikest of our poets to Shakspere. His poems, I know, are very sensuous and indeed they are sensual. This sensuality is their fault, but I do not see that it makes them feminine. But at any rate (and the second point includes the first) in this fault he resembles, not differs from Shakspere. For Keats died very young and we have only the work of his first youth. Now if we compare that with Shakspere's early work, written at an age considerably more than Keats's, was it not? such as *Venus and Adonis* and *Lucrece*, it is, as far as the work of two very original minds ever can be, greatly like in its virtues and its vices; more like, I do think, than that of any writer you could quote after the Elizabethan age; which is what the common opinion asserts. It may be that Keats was no dramatist (his *Otho* I have not seen); but it is not for that, I think, that people have made the comparison. The *Cap and Bells* is an unhappy performance, so bad that I could not get through it; senselessly planned to have no plan and doomed to fail; but Keats would have found out that. He was young; his genius intense in its quality; his feeling for beauty, for perfection intense; he had found his way right in his Odes; he would find his way right at last to the true functions of his mind. And he was at a great disadvantage in point of education compared with Shakspere. Their classical attainments may have been much of a muchness, but Shakspere had the school of his age. It was the Renaissance: the ancient Classics were deeply and enthusiastically studied and influenced directly or indirectly all, and the new learning had entered into a fleeting but brilliant combination with the medieval tradition. All then used the same forms and keepings. But in Keats's time, and worst in England, there was no one school; but experiment, division, and uncertainty. He was one of the beginners of the Romantic movement, with the extravagance and ignorance of his youth. After all is there anything in *Endymion* worse than the passage in *Romeo and Juliet* about the County Paris as a book of love that must be bound and I can't tell what? It has some kind of fantastic beauty, like an arabesque; but in the main it is nonsense. And about the true masculine fibre in Keats's mind Matthew Arnold has written something good lately.[2]

(from a letter of Gerard Manley Hopkins to Canon Dixon, 20 October 1887: text from *The Correspondence of G. M. Hopkins and R. W. Dixon*, ed. Claude Collier Abbott, 1935)

NOTES

1. The issue of 28 June 1887. The criticism is reprinted in *Principle in Art*.
2. The preface to the selection from Keats in Ward's *English Poets*, IV (1880; reprinted in *Essays in Criticism*, second series, 1888).

MATTHEW ARNOLD: 'Beauty, truth and joy'

... The thing to be seized is that Keats had flint and iron in him, that he had character; that he was, as his brother George says, 'as much like the Holy Ghost as *Johnny Keats*', – as that imagined sensuous weakling, the delight of the literary circles of Hampstead.... But indeed nothing is more remarkable in Keats than his clear-sightedness, his lucidity; and lucidity itself is akin to character and to high and severe work. In spite, therefore, of his overpowering feeling for beauty, in spite of his sensuousness, in spite of his facility, in spite of his gift of expression, Keats could say resolutely: —

'I know nothing, I have read nothing; and I mean to follow Solomon's directions: "Get learning, get understanding". There is but one way for me. The road lies through application, study, and thought. I will pursue it.' ...

The truth is that 'the yearning passion for the Beautiful', which was with Keats, as he himself truly says, the master-passion, is not a passion of the sensuous or sentimental man, is not a passion of the sensuous or sentimental poet. It is an intellectual and spiritual passion. It is 'connected and made one', as Keats declares that in his case it was, 'with the ambition of the intellect'. It is, as he again says, 'the mighty *abstract idea* of Beauty in all things'. And in his last days Keats wrote: 'If I should die, I have left no immortal work behind me – nothing to make my friends proud of my memory; *but I have loved the principle of beauty in all things*, and if I had had time I would have made myself remembered.' He *has* made himself remembered, and remembered as no merely sensuous poet could be; and he has done it by having 'loved the principle of beauty in all things'.

For to see things in their beauty is to see things in their truth, and Keats knew it. 'What the imagination seizes as Beauty must be Truth,' he says in prose; and in immortal verse he has said the same thing—

> Beauty is truth, truth beauty, – that is all
> Ye know on earth, and all ye need to know.

No, it is not all; but it is true, deeply true, and we have deep need to know it. And with beauty goes not only truth, joy goes with her also; and this too Keats saw and said, as in the famous first line of his *Endymion* it stands written—

A thing of beauty is a joy forever.

It is no small thing to have so loved the principle of beauty as to perceive the necessary relation of beauty with truth, and of both with joy....

But he had terrible bafflers – consuming disease and early death.... Nevertheless, let and hindered as he was, and with a short term and imperfect experience, – 'young', as he says of himself, 'and writing at random, straining after particles of light in the midst of a great darkness, without knowing the bearing of any one assertion, of any one opinion', – notwithstanding all this, by virtue of his feeling for beauty and of his perception of the vital connection of beauty with truth, Keats accomplished so much in poetry, that in one of the two great modes by which poetry interprets, in the faculty of naturalistic interpretation, in what we call natural magic, he ranks with Shakespeare. 'The tongue of Kean,' he says in an admirable criticism of that great actor and of his enchanting elocution, 'the tongue of Kean must seem to have robbed the Hybla bees and left them honeyless. There is an indescribable *gusto* in his voice; – in *Richard*, "Be stirring with the lark to-morrow, gentle Norfolk!" comes from him as through the morning atmosphere towards which he yearns.' This magic, this 'indescribable *gusto* in the voice', Keats himself, too, exhibits in his poetic expression. No one else in English poetry, save Shakespeare, has in expression quite the fascinating felicity of Keats, his perfection of loveliness. 'I think,' he said humbly, 'I shall be among the English poets after my death.' He is; with Shakespeare.

(from *Essays in Criticism*, second series, London and New York, 1888; reprinted from Ward's *English Poets*, IV, 1880).

VI.

THE ODES

HAD Keats *left us only his* Odes, *his rank among the poets would not be lower than it is, for they hav stood apart in literature, at least the six most famous of them; and these were all written in his best period, when he was under the* Miltonic *influence—that is, between the early spring of 1819, while he was still engag'd on* Hyperion, *and the autumn, when he discarded it.* These *are the six*: *1.* Psyche; *2.* Melancholy; *3.* Nightingale; *4.* Greek Urn; *5.* Indolence; *6.* Autumn.

To *these should be added 7, the fragment of the* May Ode, May *1, 1818, and 8, the* Ode to Pan, *from* Endymion, *bk. i, and 9, the* Bacchic Ode to Sorrow *in* Endymion, *bk. iv.* But *the two hymns to* Neptune *and* Diana *in* Endymion *are only worth enumeration, and the two early odes to* Apollo *and the* Ode to a Lock of Milton's Hair *are, as are the two later* Odes to Fanny, *chiefly or entirely of personal interest.*

Of *the seven odes first enumerated, if we rank them merely according to perfection of workmanship, the one that*

CRITICAL INTRODUCTION

was last written, that is, the Ode to Autumn, *will cleim the hĭhest place; and unless it be objected as a slĭht blemish that the words* 'Think not of them' *in the 2nd lĭne of the 3rd stanza are somewhat awkwardly address'd to a personification of* Autumn, *I do not know that eny sort of favlt can be favnd in it. But this ode does not in eny part of it reach the marvellous hĭhts attein'd bĭ several of the others in their best places, and even if judg'd as a whole it is left far behĭnd bĭ the splendour of the* Nightingale, *in which the mood is more intense, and the poetry vĭes in richness and varĭety with its subject.*

The soŋ of the nĭhtingale is, to the hearer, full of assertion, promis, and cheerful expectancy, and of pleadiŋ and tender passionat overflowiŋ in loŋ dravn-avt notes, interspersed with plenty of plɑyfulness and conscious exhibitions of musical skill. Whatever pein or sorrow mɑy be express'd bĭ it, it is ĭdealĭs'd—that is, it is not the sorrow of a sufferer, but the perfect expression of sorrow bĭ an artist, who must hav felt, but is not feeliŋ; and the ecstasy of the nĭhtingale is stronger than its sorrow, ɑltho' different hearers mɑy be differently affected accordiŋ to their mood. Keats in a sad mood seized on the happy interpretation and promis of it, and givs it in this lĭne—

> *Singest of* summer *in full-throated ease.*

KEATS

But the intense feeliŋ in his description of human sorrow (stanza 3) is weaken'd bẏ the direct platitude that the bird has never known it; and in the penultimat stanza the thavht is fanciful or superficial,—man beiŋ as immortal as the bird in every sense but that of samness, which is assumed and does not satisfẏ. The introduction, too, of the last stanza is artificial, whẏle his choosiŋ self *for a rhẏme-word,*[1] *turns avt disastrously; and he loses hold of his mɛin ẏdea in the words 'plaintive anthem', which, in expressiŋ the dẏiŋ awɛy of the savnd, changes its character. No prɛise, havever, coud be too hẏh for those last six lẏnes; and if grammar and sense are a little obscure in the first ten, I coud not name ɛny* English *poem of the same leŋth which contɛins so much beauty as this ode.*

Next to this I should rank Melancholy. *The perception in this ode is profavnd, and no davbt experienced. The paradox that melancholy is most deeply felt by the organisation most capable of joy is clinch'd at the end bẏ the observation of the reaction which satẏety provokes in such temperaments, so that it is avlso in the moment of extremest joy that it suddenly fades—*

[1] *The elf beloŋs to* W. *Brown of* Tavistock, *whom I suspect to hav been the remote cavse of the bitch in the first stanza—*

Philomel, I do not envy thy sweet carolling.

Brit. Past., *i. 3, 164.*

CRITICAL INTRODUCTION

> *Turning to poison while the bee mouth sips:*
> *Ay, in the very temple of* Delight
> *Veil'd* Melancholy *has her sovran shrine.*

In spite of the grat beauty of this ode, especially of the last stanza, it does not hit so hard as one would expect. I do not know whether this is due to a false note[1] *towards the end of the second stanza, or to a disagreement between the second and third stanzas. In the second stanza the melancholy is, as* Lord Houghton *said, a 'luxurious tenderness', while in the third it is strong, peinful, and incurable.*

The line—

> *That fosters the droop-headed flowers all,*

means all the flowers only that are sacred to sorrow. See End. *iv. 170.*

Next *in order might come* Psyche, *for the sake of the last section (l. 50 to end), tho' this is open to the objection that the imagery is work'd up to outface the idea—which is characteristic of* Keats' *manner. Yet the extreme beauty quenches every dissatisfaction. The beginning of this ode is not so good, and the middle part is midway in excellence.*

Next, *and disputing place with the last, comes the* Grecian Urn. *The thought as enounced in the first stanza is the supremacy of ideal art over* Nature, *because of its*

[1]*For its explanation, see p. 163.*

unchanging expression of perfection; and this is true and beautiful; but its amplification in the poem is unprogressiv, monotonous, and scatter'd, the attention being call'd to fresh deteils without result (see espec. ll. 21-24, anticipated in 15, 16), which givs an effect of poverty in spite of the beauty. The last stanza enters stumbling on a pun, but its concluding lines are very fine, and make a sort of recovery with their forcible directness.

The last of the six, Indolence, *is the objectiv picturing of a transient mood, and may be the description of an actual half-waking vision. If the deteils, such as the appearing of the figures four times, hav no definit meaning, and I cannot fix eny, they are too arbitrary. Parts of stanzas 2 and 3 and all the 5th are of the best work; but the whole ode scarcely earns its title; and its mein interest, that is, its fervour and feeling, betrays the poet into an undignifi'd utterance in line 4 of the last verse.*

The fragment of the May Ode *is immortal on account of the famous passag of inimitable beauty descriptiv of the Greek poets—*

> *Leaving great verse unto a little clan, etc.*

With these seven the two chief odes in Endymion *are worthy to rank. The ode to Pan in Book I is good enough in design. Pan is first invok'd as ruler in dark and moist woods;*

secondly, as the god to whom all natural products are sacred with contrast of sunny places; thirdly, as kiŋ of fawns and satyrs; fourthly, for six lines as farm-god. But *this last idea has been anticipated bi interpolation in the previous section.* Then *the last part of the ode connects* Pan *with the secrets and power of* Nature. The *expression* But no more, *however interpreted, is unfortunat at the end of the ode.* The *diction thru' out is rich and the imagery chosen well for the work that it has to do in the various aspects of the god's energy, the different objects beiŋ seized and shown in happy phrases full of knowledg and feeliŋ; and tho' it might perhaps hav been better if the second section had immediatly preceded the last, rather than that the mysteries should follow close on the farm, there is no grat favlt to find.* But *yet the ode does not at first readiŋ make an impression corresponding to these merits, nor has it won, like the others, a high reputation; and this may be due partly to the vagness of the personification, caused bi the variety of attributes and objects, and partly to the versification, which, tho' generally easy and fluent, pauses, especially in the second division, too frequently in the mid-line, in the manner of taggiŋ, and produces thare somethiŋ of the effect of a catalog, very foreign to the repose and finish which we look for in a set ode.*

KEATS

Lastly, *as to the* Ode to Sorrow *in the 4th book of* Endymion, *I regard this as one of the gratest of* Keats' *achievements, and agree with all that* Mr. Sidney Colvin *has said in its preise in his* Life of Keats. It *unfortunatly halts in the openiŋ, and the 1st and 4th stanzas especially are unequal to the rest, as is agein the 3rd from the end, '*Young *stranger', which for its matter would with more propriety hav been cast into the previous section; and these impoverish the effect, and contein expressions which might put some readers off.* If *they would begin at the 5th stanza and omit the 3rd from the end, they would find little that is not admirable.* And, *as it stands, the ode is, I think, the better for these omissions.* The *pictorial description of the* Bacchic *procession is unmatch'd for life, wide motion, and romantic dreamy* Orientalism, *while the concludiŋ stanzas, returniŋ to the first movement, are as lovely as eny* Elizabethan *lyric, and in the same manner.* The *bold contrast and passion of the ode, in spite of its weaker openiŋ and the few expressions which remind one that it is an early work, giv it a unique place amoŋ the richest creations of the* English Muse.

SOURCE: *Collected Essays, Papers, etc., of Robert Bridges, IV: A Critical Introduction to Keats.* Oxford University Press, Humphrey Milford, London, 1929. Written for the Muses Library (Keats) and sold separately in a limited edition (250), Lawrence & Buller, 1895. Reprinted and revised in *Poetical Works of John Keats,* Hodder & Stoughton, 1916.

PART THREE

Recent Studies

H. W. Garrod

THE CLOSE CONNECTIONS OF THOUGHT IN THE SPRING ODES (1926)

The question of priority in time as between the different odes which Keats composed in 1819 is one which the data are insufficient for determining; and since it is one of very little importance, I will leave it to be investigated by talents born for such inquiry. It is more important to observe the close connections of thought which exist between all of the six great Odes with the exception of that 'To Autumn' (which we know to have been written towards the end of September). Just as each Ode is something in the nature of a sonnet-sequence, so the Odes, taken together, are a sequence; an ode-sequence of which the relations, not of time, but of mood, to some extent disclose themselves. I have taken 'Psyche' to be the first in time of the Odes: and in mood also I think it begins them.

The source of Keats' knowledge of the Psyche legend I am not so well able as others to guess; nor, if I could guess it, do I suppose that it would bring me any nearer to the very individual sentiment which Keats has thrown about the legend. The appeal of Psyche to him is not more her 'loveliness' than her lateness. Of the 'faded' Olympian 'hierarchy' she is latest-born, of divinities that have all passed into unreality the least real, the most a 'vision'. 'Too late for antique vows', for a poetry of faith – 'the believing lyre' – her fascination for her poet is that he himself creates her. Not any substance in the deity herself, but his own eyes, furnish his inspiration:

> I see and sing, *by my own eyes inspir'd.*

To the creation of these inspired eyes there is promised

a worship melancholy and languorous enough. Keats will be the priest of Psyche, priest and choir and shrine and grove; she shall have a fane 'in some untrodden region of the mind', and shall enjoy

> all soft delight
> That shadowy thought can win

There shall be a 'bright torch' burning for her, and the casement shall be open to let her in at night. I do not find that any commentator has seized the significance of this symbolism. The open window and the lighted torch – they are to admit and attract the timorous *moth-goddess,* who symbolizes melancholic love.

For this is the deity which these inspired eyes have created. It is only when we come to the last lines with their

> bright torch, and a casement ope at night
> To let the warm love in

that we realize that Keats has in fact identified the Psyche who is the soul (love's soul) with the Psyche which means *moth.*[1]

It is a strange goddess whom he has thus brought from her native unrealities into the reality of the imagination. But her identity is certain – we encounter her again, brought into darker shadow, in the 'Ode on Melancholy'. The last stanza of 'Psyche' – the moth stanza – should be read in close connection with the first stanza of this (I take it) later Ode.

There is a deeper melancholy than Melancholy itself. Lethe and wolfs-bane and the deadly nightshade and the yewberry – emblems of sadness fetched from the world of flowers – are emblems only meagre and inadequate; in the world, again, of living creatures, the beetle, the owl, the moth, fall short of that for which we invoke their symbolism:

Nor let the beetle, *nor the death-moth be*
Your mournful Psyche, nor the downy owl
A partner in your sorrow's mysteries;
For shade to shade will come too drowsily,
And drown the wakeful anguish of the soul.

There is the same identification here (only clearer) of Psyche and the moth – here called the *death-moth*. This moth-goddess, this 'mournful Psyche', who typifies melancholic love, even if we conceive the melancholy passion wrought to that degree that it is symbolized by the *death-moth*,[2] is no partner in the mysteries of that deeper and truer Melancholy which the Ode celebrates. It is the paradox of this deeper Melancholy that she dwells with beauty, that she has her 'sovran shrine' 'in the very temple of Delight',[3] though, like the Psyche for whom the 'Ode to Psyche' builds a 'fane', she is 'seen of none' save the poet. The 'strenuous tongue' of the poet, his courage of eloquence, which tries all sweets of the sense upon its palate, alone 'can burst Joy's grape', and taste the heart of Melancholy:

His soul shall taste the sadness of her might,
And be among her cloudy trophies hung.[4]

It is hateful to hunt a moral. But to suppose Keats (or any other poet) to say so much, and to mean nothing of it – or, indeed, less than all of it – is to save poetry out of ethics at too great a price. I suppose him to mean all of it; though that is not to say that he has developed the mood consciously – for so perhaps it would be, not poetry, but prose – or that he is to be detained in it permanently, as though poetry had not many mansions. But I suppose him to say, and to mean, not merely that the poet has a more delicate perception than common men of the beauty of the world of sense, a 'finer palate' for joy; and not merely that this delicate perception is intensified in him by the consciousness (which, again, is deeper in him than in others) that the perfections of sense are born and perish in the same moment; not merely that; but that the top of poetry, its supreme mood, is precisely that mood in which the beauty, of which the poet is priest and worshipper, is so apprehended that the awareness of it is *anguish* – a 'wakeful anguish', in comparison with which all other dark effects which meet in the soul come together as 'shade to shade', 'drowsily' and listlessly, mere melancholic fits of lovesick or repining men.

By the grace of God these supreme moments of poetry are rare, these times when the soul is so truly captivated by beauty, by that paradox of simultaneous unfolding and fading which constitutes the glory of the sensuous world, that she is left a trophy hung in the shrine of impenetrable sadness; these times are rare. For the most part, our poetry, like our love, is not more than a 'drowsy' sentiency:

> For shade to shade will come too drowsily,
> And drown the wakeful anguish of the soul,

that wakeful anguish which *is* poetry.

'Too drowsily.' Keats likes the word, and the idea. The *idea* pervades the Psyche Ode. Upon the *word*, the 'Ode to a Nightingale' opens:

> My heart aches, and a *drowsy numbness pains*
> My sense, ...

It is used twice in the 'Ode on Indolence':

> Ripe was the *drowsy* hour;
> The blissful cloud of summer indolence
> *Benumb'd* my eyes; my pulse grew less and less;
> Pain had no sting, and pleasure's wreath no flower;

and again:

> O folly! What is Love! and where is it?
> And for that poor Ambition! it springs
> From a man's little heart's short fever-fit;

For Poesy! – no, – she has not a joy,
At least for me, – so sweet as *drowsy* noons,
And evenings steeped in honied indolence.

The mood of this 'drowsy' indolence Keats calls 'my 1819 mood'. Yet from it spring, as we have also seen, not only all the great Odes, save 'Autumn', but 'The Eve of St Agnes'. The truth is that the drowsiness and indolence of Keats is the poetry of other men; indeed, the poetry of Keats himself, but that he will never be content in it. In the 'Ode on Melancholy' he conceives it as a kind of duty for the poet to keep alive in himself the anguished appreciation of beauty. If that 'wakeful anguish' be 'drowned', his insight perishes, he has stopped short of the proper and fatal consummation of the joy of the senses.

This is only the old scepticism about the senses finding for itself a new direction. Out of that luxury of sensation, which is his true effectiveness, Keats must be for ever scheming himself into some unhappiness; now he runs from sense to thought, to metaphysical reflection; now from mere poetry to a poetry of social suffering; and, yet again here, he is not happy till he can discover in the joy of the senses themselves – without the need to go outside them – not unhappiness, merely, but some fated and immortal anguish. If he cannot flee from the pure enjoyment of the beautiful, he can yet perish in it.

Perhaps there is more of Keats in this perverse ingenuity of the 'Ode on Melancholy' than in the rather formal philosophy (if philosophy it be) of the 'Ode on a Grecian Urn'. The 'Grecian Urn' we may suppose to have been written in a mood of strong revulsion from the thesis of 'Melancholy'. 'Melancholy' remains fixed courageously, almost defiantly, in the gospel of the senses, ready to die for, and in, it. It

dwells with Beauty, Beauty that must die,
And Joy whose hand is ever at his lips
Bidding adieu.

It is the world of the poet, though he perish in it. The 'Grecian Urn' presents, in fact, the same world, the world of beauty and human passions, only fixed by art. The lover whom the Urn figures loves, not a 'beauty that must die', but that which, from the nature of art, 'cannot fade'. The song that he sings he sings 'not to the sensual ear', but 'to the spirit',

> All breathing human passion far above,
> That leaves a heart high-sorrowful and cloyed,
> A burning forehead and a parching tongue.

The first four stanzas of the Ode achieve a faultless harmonization of thought, sentiment, and language. But I have never been able to think the last stanza worthy of the rest, or consistent with it. It begins badly, in diction. I dislike, as much as Mr Bridges does, the assonance *Attic ... attitude,* in the first line of it, and the obscurely intended affectation 'brede'. I dislike, in the fifth line, the metrical carry-over 'As doth Eternity' – this is the only place in the Ode where a clear separation is not maintained between quatrain and sestet. In lines 7–8 the metrical carry-over 'in midst of other woe Than ours ...' is, I think, almost equally objectionable – though the pause after it is less full. Indeed, the movement of the whole of the sestet is 'choppy'. But more serious than any of these faults – and a fault of which these are symptomatic – the connections of the stanza both internally and in respect of the stanzas preceding are difficult. The theme of what has gone before is the arrest of beauty, the fixity given by art to forms which in life are fluid and impermanent, and the appeal of art from the senses to the spirit. The theme of the final stanza is the relation of beauty to truth, to thought. Nothing has prepared the transition to this. The first half of the stanza, moreover, makes it the effect of art, of this '*cold* pastoral' (of which, none the less, the loves are 'forever warm'), that it 'teases us out of thought, as doth Eternity'. Yet the effect upon which our attention has hitherto been concentrated is that the Urn lifts us out of sense into thought, or at least into 'the spirit' (stanza ii, lines 3–4). What has happened? The beholder, I suppose, kept so long from sense in the region of thought, is now assailed by misgivings about the reality of a work of art thus remote from the warm breathing life of the sensible world. The figures of the Urn become for him, suddenly, a '*cold* Pastoral' – cold with the character of everything that is enduring. In comparison with the warm human world that he knows, what reality have these figured creations? The second half of the stanza – of which the first, marring seriously, as I think, the effect of all that has preceded, has called in question the appeal of ideal art – the second half of the stanza seeks to allay the doubt set up; to allay it by the thesis that there is nothing real but the beautiful, and nothing beautiful but the real.

I find these difficulties, then, in this final stanza. I find them there, I know, by subjecting the verses to a greater rigour of analysis than is just to such a context. But every reader, I think, in some degree feels them, feels a certain uneasiness; and I have not sought to do more than discover the ground of this uneasiness. The lines *are* difficult; they do not, either in thought or feeling, hang true with the rest of the Ode. More than that I would not urge. Down to the end of the fourth stanza there is a very perfect development of the governing idea – 'the supremacy of ideal art over nature, because of its unchanging expression of perfection'.[5] Perhaps the fourth stanza is more beautiful than any of the others – and more true. The trouble is that it is a little too true. Truth to his main theme has taken Keats rather farther than he meant to go. The pure and ideal art of this 'cold Pastoral', this 'silent form', *has* a cold silentness which in some degree saddens him. In the last lines of the fourth stanza, especially the last three lines,

> And, little town, thy streets for evermore
> Will silent be; and not a soul to tell
> Why thou art desolate, can e'er return,

every reader is conscious, I should suppose, of an undertone of sadness, of disappointment. This pure and cold art makes, in fact, a less appeal to Keats than the Ode as a whole would pretend; and when, in the lines which follow these lines, he indulges the jarring apostrophe 'Cold Pastoral' (for jarring it is, – we detect, do what we may, some accidental undertone of depreciation), he has said more than he meant – or than he wished to mean. The 'cold Pastoral' is, in fact, beginning to tease him away from thought, from these pure unchangeable ideal forms, back to some creed more like himself than the rest of the Ode.

The lines in this Ode which speak of art as teasing us out of thought echo, as I have already noticed, some lines of the Epistle to Reynolds':

Things cannot to the will
Be settled, but they tease us out of thought . . .
. It is a flaw
In happiness, to see beyond our bourn;
It forces us in summer nights to mourn,
It spoils *the singing of the nightingale.*

The lines were a year old, and more, when Keats wrote the 'Grecian Urn' – and the 'Ode to a Nightingale'. The latter poem is written in the spirit of them – into the former that spirit, as we have seen, has somewhat inappositely intruded itself. There is that much connection between the two Odes: and between the 'Nightingale Ode' and 'Melancholy' a closer connection. In the 'Ode on Melancholy', whatever is beautiful in the world is 'spoilt' by something in the nature of our apprehension of it – or rather, of the poet's apprehension of it; by something which is, indeed, in the nature of beauty, of which the true apprehension is anguish. In the 'Nightingale Ode', the singing of the Nightingale is spoilt, not by any anguish which there is in its joy, its 'happiness', its 'ecstasy', but, as in the lines to Reynolds, by the intrusion of a *human* trouble – in the lines to Reynolds, it is the trouble of abstract thought, in the 'Ode to a Nightingale' the trouble of suffering humanity. But it is not accident, I fancy, whereby 'Melancholy' opens with its

> No, no, go not to Lethe, –

Lethe, where the shades of sorrow come 'too drowsily' – and the 'Ode to a Nightingale' upon its note of 'drowsy numbness', its mood of sinking 'Lethe-wards':

> My heart aches, and a *drowsy numbness* pains
> My sense, as though of hemlock I had drunk,
> Or emptied some dull opiate to the drains
> One minute past, and *Lethe-wards had sunk.*

This heart-ache and drowsy numbness, this sinking Lethe wards, proceed, 'not from envy of' the 'happy lot' of the Nightingale, but from the poet's sense of 'being too happy in its happiness'. This happiness, this mere joy in what is beautiful, seems – as it has so often seemed to him before – 'a crime'; 'and yet I must'. He surrenders himself to the spell of it; and it is interesting to observe the subtle shading off of mood into mood as the Ode develops itself stanza by stanza:

> But being too happy in thine happiness,
> That thou, light-winged Dryad of the trees,
> In some melodious plot.[6]
> Of beechen green and shadows numberless,
> Singest of summer in full-throated ease.

I suppose every poet takes the intoxication of his own words. The 'beechen green and shadows numberless' carry Keats' imagination to dim faraway forests into which he would gladly, 'leaving the world, unseen' fade away. But the development of the idea is delayed over a whole stanza by another phrase. 'Singest of summer in full-throated ease': a phrase which dictates the immediately following:

O for a draught of vintage! that hath been
Cool'd a long age in the deep-delved earth ...

with all the luxury of description that succeeds, all so 'full of the warm south':

That I might drink, and leave the world unseen,
And with thee fade away into the forest dim:

But these closing lines of a stanza so rich in sensuous beauty have fallen upon a melancholy rhythm; and again the infection of his own accidents of style, if I may so call them, compels the direction of thought; the rhythm and words together determine the stanza which comes next:

And with thee *fade away* into the forest dim:

Fade far away, dissolve, and quite forget[7]
What thou among the leaves hast never known,
The weariness, the fever, and the fret,
Here, where men sit, and hear each other groan,
Where palsy shakes a few, sad, last gray hairs,
Where youth grows pale, and spectre-thin, and dies;
Where but to think is to be full of sorrow,
And leaden-eyed despairs,
Where Beauty cannot keep her lustrous eyes,
Or new love pine at them beyond tomorrow.

The temperament 'too happy in happiness' has drawn here dangerously near to that which dictated the '*Ode on Melancholy*':

She dwells with Beauty – Beauty that must die;
And Joy, whose hand is ever at his lips
Bidding adieu;

and the 'Away! away!' that introduces the fourth stanza is inevitable – an inevitable revulsion:

Away! away! for I will fly to thee,
Not charioted by Bacchus and his pards,[8]
But on the viewless wings of poesy,
Though the dull brain perplexes and retards:

The 'dull brain', 'the meddling intellect', as Wordsworth calls it, is not to be allowed to tease him into thought. 'Already with thee!', he says confidently. The night is 'tender', the moon enthroned, with her court of stars about her; and by this time we suppose our poet to be where are all these splendours of light and song. But no. Not 'the dull brain', but the very senses themselves have drawn him back to earth. The moon is on her throne:

But here there is no light,
Save what from heaven is with the breezes blown
Through verdurous glooms and winding mossy ways.

The luxury of these 'verdurous glooms', their 'embalmed darkness', detains him, guessing 'each sweet'.

I cannot see what flowers are at my feet,
Nor what soft incense hangs upon the boughs,
But in embalmed darkness, guess each sweet
Wherewith the seasonable month endows
The grass, the thicket, and the fruit-tree wild;
White hawthorn, and the pastoral eglantine,
Fast fading violets cover'd up in leaves;
And mid-May's eldest child,
The coming musk-rose, full of dewy wine,
The murmurous haunt of flies on summer eves.

That 'exquisite sense of the luxurious', in which he could not persuade himself that he was even moderately qualified, has here taken direction of the whole poem. Among these sweets of sense, it seems 'rich to die', to make of death itself a kind of sensuous luxury:

To cease upon the midnight with no pain,

While thou art pouring forth thy soul abroad
In such an ecstasy!
Still would'st thou sing, and I have ears in vain –
To thy high requiem become a sod.

To the stanza that follows I do not feel the objection that Mr Bridges alleges, who finds the thought 'fanciful or artificial', 'man being as immortal as the bird in every sense but that of sameness, which is assumed and does not satisfy'.[9] On the other hand, Miss Lowell only answers this objection by not seeing the point of it. 'In calling the nightingale "immortal bird",' she writes, 'and contrasting its eternity of life with man's short existence, any one with a spark of imaginative or poetic feeling realises at once that Keats is not referring to the particular nightingale singing at that instant, but to the species nightingale.' How people behave who have 'a spark of imaginative or poetic feeling', I would, for my part, rather learn from Mr Bridges than from Miss Lowell. Except for Mr Bridges, Miss Lowell would 'not stoop', she tells us, 'to the primer-like explanation'. Primer-like it perhaps is. It is like a bad primer; not merely the teacher, that is, but the child, can see that it is absurd. The species nightingale is just as much, or just as little, immortal as the species man. Nor is it necessary, though nearer to sense, and certainly ingenious, to say with Sir Sidney Colvin that 'what Keats has in mind is not the song-bird at all, but the bird-song, thought of as though it were a thing self-existing and apart, imperishable through the ages'.[10] What Keats has in mind *is* 'the particular nightingale singing at that instant'. This 'light-winged Dryad of the trees' is, like all other Dryads – and Naiads, and all Nymphs and fays – like all the people of Faery, all the lesser divinities of the classical library – immortal. *This* nightingale, and not the species merely to which it belongs, was 'not born for death'. *This* nightingale, and not some other of its kind, was heard 'in ancient days' by I know not what 'emperor and clown'. Has Keats fallen on some confused recollection of *Lear*?

'The foul fiend haunts poor Tom in the voice of a nightingale,' says Edgar to Lear and the fool. For Edgar, it is true, the Dryad has turned devil, the fay is the foul fiend.

Whence Keats fetched, in this stanza, the thought of Ruth, Ruth 'in tears amid the alien corn', it is idle to conjecture. It is just this divine inconsequence of poetry which makes its reasoning more consecutive than reason. But I have the fancy, for what it is worth, that the image of Ruth amid the corn came to Keats, by some obscure process of association, from Wordsworth's *Solitary Reaper*:

> Alone she cuts and binds the grain,
> And sings a melancholy strain.
> O listen, for the vale profound
> Is overflowing with the sound!
>
> No Nightingale did ever chant
> So sweetly to reposing bands
> Of travellers in some shady haunt
> Amid Arabian sands.
>
> No sweeter voice was ever heard
> In springtime from the cuckoo-bird,
> Breaking the silence of the seas
> Among the farthest Hebrides.
>
> Will no one tell me what she sings?
> Perhaps the plaintive numbers flow
> For old unhappy far-off things,
> And battles long ago.

What parts of this affecting music and imagery faint airs of memory may have borne to Keats' mind, I would not care to inquire too curiously. Some part, I think; and I would even hazard the conjecture that the 'plaintive numbers' of Wordsworth's poem – just that phrase, lingering unaccountably – caused Keats to strike the only false note which the Ode discovers:

Adieu! adieu! thy plaintive anthem fades.

'He loses hold of his main idea in the words *plaintive anthem*', says Mr Bridges, truly.[11] Not plaint, but 'ecstasy', 'happiness', 'full-throated ease', is the quality of the Nightingale's singing, as Keats hears it in the other stanzas. But Wordsworth, as I fancy, has carried him out of his 'main idea'; Wordsworth, and also, it may be, once again, the infection of his own rhythms – the rhythms in which the penultimate stanza closes:

The same that oft-times hath
Charm'd magic casements, opening on the foam
Of perilous seas, in faery lands forlorn.

Whether these verses owe anything to Wordsworth's cuckoo-song,

Breaking the silence of the seas
Amid the furthest Hebrides,

I will not ask; they at least owe more to Wordsworth than – where Miss Lowell finds a debt – to Diodorus Siculus![12] But the melancholy cadence of them, Keats felt himself. He takes up the last word, and makes it the first word, and the key-word, of the stanza following:

Forlorn! the very word is like a bell
To toll me back from thee to my sole self!

Mr Bridges finds the transition 'artificial'. That I do not feel; nor do I feel that the six final verses of the Ode deserve all the praise that Mr Bridges gives them. 'No praise could be too high', he says, 'for those last six verses.' That praise, I think, is. Both of this Ode and of the 'Ode on a Grecian Urn' I think the close not wholly worthy of the rest. In both poems, the last stanza seems to me to 'lose hold of the main idea', and to suffer at the same time a deterioration of rhythmical effect.

SOURCE: *Keats: Lectures from the Oxford Chair of Poetry*, 1926.

NOTES

1. The Greek word means both 'soul' and 'moth' or 'butterfly'. In works of art, Psyche is sometimes represented as a butterfly.
2. The name death-moth Keats seems to have invented. It stands, no doubt, for the death's-head moth (*Acherontia atropos*). The word is formed, presumably, on the analogy of death-worm or death-watch, the creature which he calls the beetle (*Atropos pulsatorius*). The 'death-watch' is mentioned in *Endymion*, iv 531—and derives, perhaps, from Wordsworth, *Excursion*, iv 617. The nightshade, which he also mentions, is sometimes called death's-herb.
3. The general idea is anticipated in *A Song of Opposites* ('Welcome Joy').
4. The poet's soul, it is perhaps worth noticing, is figured here as one of the ornaments of the temple of Melancholy, just as, in the 'Ode to Psyche', the poet is the lute and pipe and 'chain-swung censer' in the 'fane' of Psyche.
5. Bridges, *A Critical Introduction to the Poems of John Keats*, p. lxvi.
6. The transference of epithet in this bold and happy phrase is notable. Similar, and equally bold and happy, is, in the fourth stanza, 'no light, Save what from heaven is with the breezes *blown*'—.
7. *Quite to forget* Earth's turmoils, spights, and wrongs – Drummond, 'To a Nightingale' (*Flowers of Sion*, xxiii 11). But the coincidence is, I am sure fortuitous.
8. As an illustration of the want of attention – and of knowledge – with which poetry is so often read, I cannot resist putting upon record here a rendering of this line in Latin elegiacs, which I was once shown: Non *Bacchi comtes*, non deus ipse duces (*comites*, 'pards', 'partners')!
9. Op. cit., p. lxiv.

10. *Life*, p. 419.
11. Op. cit., p. lxiv.
12. 'perilous seas' has replaced, in Keats' MS., something else – which the editors read as 'keelless seas'. I have seen only the facsimile of the MS. But 'keelless' certainly does not correspond with the *ductus litterarum*; and I could wish that a good palaeographer should re-examine the MS.

M. R. Ridley

THE COMPOSITION OF 'NIGHTINGALE' (1933)

Sir Sidney Colvin's general account of the draft of 'Ode to a Nightingale' is as follows: 'There are many vital corrections and alterations; with frequent signs, in the shape of dropped words and letters, unaccustomed mis-spellings and slips of the pen, that while the hand wrote the mind was too much occupied with the act of composition to guide it with strict care.' In fact there are eleven cases of omitted letters (seven of which are *r*, which is always liable to drop out with Keats) and four are unwanted letters; of mis-spellings there are three, 'told' and 'feaver' both immediately corrected, and 'Emperour' (if that is a mis-spelling); there are fourteen verbal corrections of which ten are just Woodhouse's 'word here or there preferable to an expression already used'. Of the remaining four, two, because they involve rhyme words, and two because of the way in which they were made, were evidently made in the process of 'composition or recomposition', and there are six false starts. It is impossible to find any seven consecutive stanzas, or for that matter any seven stanzas at all, in the holograph of 'The Eve of St Agnes' which show so low a proportion of corrections made in the act of composition. A mere glance at the two documents would convince any one that they probably belong to different stages in composition. However, let us take the draft as we have it, and assume either that it is the first draft (in which case I think that it is a miracle, and a miracle quite different in the methods of its wizardry from Keats' usual methods where we can see them) or that it is an early draft, probably a re-writing of the first rough draft at a very short interval after the composition of that rough draft while the poem was still partially fluid, and let us go on to what is I believe in all the Odes a much more interesting study than their 'carpentry', namely the process of what one may call 'distillation' whereby many 'flowers' that we find scattered about in Keats' own earlier work, and in the work of others, together with impressions made upon his senses, are made to yield their concentrated essence. One caveat should perhaps be entered at once. In this region it is impossible to produce any evidence. We know the goal, and we are pursuing a highly conjectural backward trail; occasionally we come on a blaze which seems to be unmistakable, but even so it is no more than an encouragement to proceed on what is to some readers a fascinating adventure and to others the merest waste of time. 'Why', they will say, changing the metaphor, 'trouble our heads as to what odd lumps of ore went into the crucible when we know how pure the gold is that came out?'

His dramatic sense prevents Keats starting with the nightingale; the stage must be set, however briefly, and he sets it by a description of his own sensations, his heartache and a painful numbness. It is the same feeling perhaps that he has described to Bailey in a letter of the preceding year: 'I have this morning such a Lethargy that I cannot write ... and yet it is an unpleasant numbness it does not take away the pain of existence.'[1] The first line read originally I think

Heart aches and a painful numbness fall

(*Aches* being Shakespeareanly a dissyllable) and then

My heart aches and a drowsy numbness falls

and then, with the transference of the idea of pain into the verb, the line as we now have it

My heart aches and a drowsy numbness pains

The change may have been due to no more than trouble with rhyme, but it is observable that both *ache* and *numbness* seem to have been associated in Keats' mind with the notion of drowsy. In stanza XXXI of 'The Eve of St Agnes' we have

Or I shall drowse beside thee, so my soul doth ache

and in the 'Ode to Indolence'

Ripe was the drowsy hour;
The blissful cloud of summer-indolence
Benumb'd my eyes (st. II)

(where also in stanza III we have *ach'd for wings*).

At any rate, the first line surmounted, the stanza moves unhaltingly to its close, with one correction, that of *hence* to *past* in the fourth line, a probable reminiscence of *Britannia's Pastorals,*[2] 'Sweet *Philomela*; ... I doe not envy thy sweet carolling', and the use of one phrase of which the sound seems to have been running in Keats' head, since in *Endymion* we find *beechen wreath,*[3] *beechen tree,*[4] and *wreathed green.*[5] Part of the effect of this stanza depends on the reiterated *um* and *un* sound, three of the recurrences of which (*some* twice and *one* once) we tend to miss, from our inveterate habit of reading by the eye and not by the ear.

In the second stanza Keats wants a draught of something which is different both in itself and in its effects from the hemlock of the first stanza, and something, perhaps the link of the *beechen wreath* and *wreathed green* phrases, takes him back to *Endymion*. Here is the material. A passage in a letter of the month before: 'And, please heaven, a little claret-wine cool out of a cellar a mile deep ... a strawberry bed to say your prayers to Flora in';[6]

Here is wine,
Alive with *sparkles* – never, I aver,
Since Ariadne was a *vintager,*
So *cool a purple* (*End.* ii. 441)
the rills

Into the wide stream came of *purple* hue
. . . .
Like to a moving *vintage* down they came,
Crown'd with green leaves (*End.* iv 194)

possibly two passages in *Endymion* in which sparkling wine is in contiguity though not connection with the *beechen wreath* phrases;[7] the title of an early poem 'A Draught of Sunshine' and a line from the same poem,

My wine *overbrims* a whole summer

another three lines from *Endymion*,

Each having a white wicker *over brimm'd*
With April's tender younglings: next, well trimm'd,
A crowd of shepherds with as *sunburnt* looks....
(*End.* i 137)

perhaps the *low delved tomb* in Milton's 'On the Death of a Fair Infant';[8] and perhaps various descriptions of Provençal country feasts and dances from Mrs Radcliffe.[9]

There are the fragments, and from them Keats creates this stanza, redolent of the country, warm with the sunshine of the South:

O for a draught of vintage that has been
Cooling an age in the deep-delved earth
Tasting of Flora, and the country green
And Dance and p[r]ovencal song and sunburnt mirth
O for a Beaker full of the warm South,
Full of the true and blushful Hippocrene
With cluster'd bubbles winking at the brim
And pu[r]ple stained mouth,
That I might drink and leave the world unseen
And with thee fade away into the forest dim.

He changed *Cooling an age* to *Cooled a long age* in

the draft. In the printed version, apart from one or two minor changes, the *cluster'd* bubbles become *beaded*. This last alteration is clearly because of the *cluster'd* in stanza IV, which he there deletes as a repetition of the word here, but finally decides to leave standing there, where indeed it is more appropriate, and so is driven to the felicitous emendation in this stanza.

He starts his next stanza with a repetition which he had already used in *Endymion, fade, and fade away*,[10] and the tone of the poem changes as he thinks of leaving the world. There is here the expression of his own longing for release that comes out so poignantly elsewhere; he wants to *dissolve* like the Spirit in *Isabella* (XLI 1) or perhaps recalls the wish that this too too solid flesh would melt, Thaw and resolve itself into a dew, and that so he could escape from the sorrows of the world. Here I think is just the vivid expression of his own feelings; he knows the weariness and fever and fret; he has watched youth grow pale and spectre-thin and die five months before; he knows the lustrous eyes of beauty and guesses that even the barren ecstasy of pining at them cannot be his beyond tomorrow. This stanza comes so clearly from the tortured heart that I do not know that we need look for the material of it otherwhere than in his experience. We can if we like turn to 'Tintern Abbey', and find

> the fretful stir
> Unprofitable, and the fever of the world

and notice the '*leaden* looks' of the sullen day in *Endymion*, i 686, 'The *lustrous* passion from a falcon *eye*' in the Song to Sorrow, and three other lines in *Endymion*,

> My fever'd parchings up, my scathing dread
> Met palsy half way: soon these limbs became
> Gaunt, wither'd sapless, feeble, cramp'd and lame
> (iii 636)

This stanza gave more trouble in the actual writing.

It moves so far easily enough.

Fade far away, dissolve and quite forget
  What thou among the leaves hast never known
The weariness, the fever and the fret
  Here, where Men sit and hear each other groan
Where palsy shakes a few sad last grey hairs
  Where youth grows pale and thin and old and dies

But that is monotonous in rhythm and not too vivid in imagery, so it is strengthened to

Where youth grows pale and spectre-thin, and dies

For the last four lines I suspect an earlier stage in which there was a rhyme for the *grief* which appears cancelled in the draft, and no *new* before *Love*. Keats then in copying wrote:

Where but to think is to be full of grief
  And leaden eyed despairs—
Where Beauty cannot keep her lustrous eyes
  Or Love pine at them

and then stopped, changed *grief* to *sorrow* (for which, after the Song to Sorrow, the rhyme was familiar), inserted *new* and wrote *beyond tomorrow*.[11]

In the fourth stanza the determination to escape becomes yet more urgent, but the agency of the second stanza is rejected, and the escape is to be on the only wings of a dove on which he knew that he could fly away and be at rest, the wings of poetry, and by the fifth line the escape is achieved, and he is with the Nightingale in the depths of the forest, a forest so dark that even the presence of the throned moon is conjectural. And in this stanza I think one can see that the use of the words *fade away* and *dissolve* has set a whole new chime ringing in his head:

thou (the moon) didst *fade, and fade away*
Yet not entirely; no, thy *starry sway*... (*End*. iii 177)

Dissolve the frozen purity of air
 ...make more bright
The *Star-Queen's* crescent on her marriage night
(*End.* iv 586 *ff*)

but rather tie
Large wings upon my shoulders,...
......by all the stars
That tend thy bidding, I do think the bars
That kept my spirit in are burst – that I
Am sailing with thee through the dizzy sky!
(*End.* ii 177–87)

Add to these perhaps Titian's picture of Bacchus and Ariadne (though the pards of Bacchus are such a commonplace that I doubt whether the picture is very relevant), and probably a passage in Coleridge's *The Nightingale* (a poem which by the way seems to have influenced a passage in *Endymion* shortly before one of those quoted above):

You see the glimmer of the stream beneath,
But hear no *murmuring*; it flows silently,
O'er its soft bed of verdure. All is still
A balmy night... (ll. 5–8)

And so comes the stanza, with that remarkable piece of imagination at the end which feels the light as blown by the breezes, one of those characteristic sudden flashes with which Keats fires the most ordinary material.

Away – Away – for I will fly with thee

but *with* which was appropriate in the *Endymion* passage is not appropriate here and is altered to *to*:

Away – Away – for I will fly to thee
 Not charioted by Bacchus and his Pards
But on the viewless wings of Poesy
 Though the dull brain perplexes and retards—

(O for a life of Sensations rather than of Thoughts)

Already with thee! tender is the night
 And haply the Queen-moon is on her throne
  Clusted around by all her starry fays –
But here there is no light
 Save what from heaven is with the breezes blown
  Sidelong

One imagines that the line originally ran either

Sidelong through verdurous glooms and mossy ways

or

Sidelong through verdurous glooms and winding ways.

But in writing this draft *Sidelong* is cancelled as soon as written. It is a favourite word with Keats[12] and he may have been resisting the temptation to overwork it, but it may be doubted whether this excision was for the better; the word gives so clear a picture of a forest so dense overhead that the only light which penetrates comes sidelong from the outskirts. Anyway for good or ill the correction was made, and the line ran

Th[r]ough ve[r]du[r]ous glooms and winding mossy ways.

And lastly *Clusted* was deleted as a repetition and nothing substituted. For the printed version, as has been pointed out, it was here reinstated and the earlier *Cluster'd* changed to *beaded.*

The next stanza runs very easily, at least at this stage, and is a piece of pure description, a distillation of many previous descriptions of which the following are typical:

there blew
Soft *breezes* from the myrtle vale below;

And brought in faintness, solemn, sweet and slow
A hymn from Dian's temple; while upswelling,
The *incense* went to her own starry dwelling,
('I stood tiptoe...' 195)
Softly the *breezes* from the forest came
Softly they blew aside the taper's flame;
Clear was the song from *Philomel's* far bower;
Grateful the *incense* from the lime-tree *flower*
('Calidore' 152)
What is more tranquil than a *musk-rose* blowing
In a green island far from all men's knowing?
More healthful than the leafiness of dales?
More secret than a nest of *nightingales*?
('Sleep and Poetry', 5)

(And perhaps a passage from *The Mysteries of Udolpho*, 'illumined only by moon-beams, which the open casement admitted ... cool and balmy air, that lightly waved the embowering honeysuckles, and wafted their sweet breath into the apartment';[13] if any reader feels that, while Mrs Radcliffe may be reluctantly admitted as a possible source of 'The Eve of St Agnes', to connect her with the 'Ode to a Nightingale' is a kind of desecration, there is worse to come.)

I cannot see what flowers are at my feet
Nor what blooms

altered at once to the far better

Nor what soft insence hangs upon the boughs
But in embalmed darkness guess each sweet
With with

immediately deleted, and the point is a trivial one enough, but worth indicating since it is so characteristic of Keats in a hurry or careless. He has either in his mind or on paper *With which*, and begins to write it, when it occurs to him that *Wherewith* will be better, and the second *with* is a jumble of *which* and *with*:

> Wherewith the seasonable month endows
> The grass the thicket and the fruit tree wild
> White Hawthorn and the pastoral eglantine
> Fast fading violets covered up in leaves
> And midmay's eldest child
> The coming muskrose full of sweetest wine
> The murmurous ha[u]nt of flies on summer eves

In the printed version *sweetest* is altered to *dewy*, a change full of interest, when we watch the progression of which it was the last step. In 'I stood tiptoe...' he speaks of *dewy roses* and perhaps the whole passage is not without interest, for here too is the withdrawal from the world, there is one familiar phrase, and another which may account for the false start of *blooms*:

> Fair *dewy roses* brush against our faces,
> And flowering laurels spring from diamond vases;
> O'er head we see the jasmine and sweet briar,
> And *bloomy* grapes laughing from green attire;
> While *at our feet*...... (133–7)

In *Endymion*, ii 983, we find *dewy balm* and ten lines lower 'I roam in pleasant *darkness*' and 'where we might Be *incense*-pillow'd every summer night'; in 'Isabella' '*dewy rhyme*' (of interest only as showing how his ear was caught by the vowel slide from *ew* to long *i*); then in 'Meg Merrilies' the last stage but one,

> Her *wine* was *dew* of the wild white rose (st. II)

and so to the stanza before us.

The next stanza resembles the third in that it is a record of Keats' own experience and his mind at the time. We have the line of a sonnet ('Why did I laugh ...' MBF, 114 (343)),

> Yet would I on this very *midnight cease*

and the conclusion of the same sonnet,

> Death is Life's high meed

There is a kind of link between the two stanzas in the sonnet to Sleep:

O soft *embalmer* of the still *midnight*
  Shutting with careful fingers and benign
Our gloom-pleas'd eyes embowered from the light

The spirit is that in which he writes to Fanny Brawne two months later, 'I have two luxuries to brood over in my walks, your Loveliness and the hour of my death'.[14] But the idea of the richness of death has been with him ever since 'Sleep and Poetry':

That I may die a death
Of luxury (58)

the idea of its quietness since *Endymion*, ii 159, 'How *quiet* death is' and both ideas together since

with a *balmy* power,
Medicined death to a lengthy *drowsiness*:
The which she fills with visions, and doth dress
In all this *quiet luxury* (*End.* ii 483–6)

Darkling I listen, and for many a time
  I have been half in love with easeful death
Call'd him soft names in many a mused rhyme,
  To take into the air my painless breath
Now, more than ever seems it rich to die
  To cease upon the midnight with no pain
    While thou(gh) art pouring thus thy soul abroad
In such an Extacy—
  Still would thou sing and I have yea[r]s in vain
    But requiem'd

The cancellation of these last two words suggests a change in the thought. It looks as though in the first conception there had been a hint of consolation,

But (nevertheless) requiem'd by thy song, even though
  a sod

The revised version is more unsparing,

For To thy high requiem, become a sod.

And now for the great stanza in which the glowing imagination is fanned to yet whiter heat, the stanza that would, I suppose, by common consent be taken, along with *Kubla Khan*, as offering us the distilled sorceries of 'Romanticism', the stanza that contains those two lines, of which, along with three from *Kubla Khan*, it has been said, 'Remember that in all the millions permitted there are no more than five – five little lines – of which one can say: "These are the pure Magic. These are the clear Vision. The rest is only poetry".'[15]

We get a hint of the same backward-throwing imagination in an early letter, where he has been looking at less poetic birds at Carisbrooke: 'I dare say I have seen many a descendant of some old cawer who peeped through the Bars at Charles the First',[16] but here he carries the imagination to its limits; the song is the same and deathless through the years, even though it were the ancestor of this particular nightingale that sang to Emperours. And there is a hint perhaps of the generations in *The Excursion*:

While man *grows old* and withers and decays
And countless *generations* of mankind
Depart and leave no vestige where they trod
(iv 760)

We need hardly look for a more recondite source for Ruth than the obvious one in the Bible. And the casements? Keats had all his life a love of windows. One of his fellow students is recorded as saying, 'In a room he was always at the window peering into space so that the window seat was spoken of by his comrades as Keats's place'. We find the love of windows opening over water in the letters, 'the Window opening upon Winander mere',[17] and 'I should like the window to open onto the Lake of Geneva';[18] and his poetry is full of casements, as in the famous stanza of 'The Eve of St Agnes' and the 'casement ope' of the 'Ode to Psyche', and the open casement of the 'Ode to Indolence'. It has been held that the genesis of the picture of the two famous lines as revised with the casements *magic* and the seas *perilous*, was Claude's picture of 'The Enchanted Castle'.[19] But what are the salient features of this picture? A castle by the sea, with plenty of casements (and *ex hypothesi* from the title of the picture, though apart from the title one would hardly guess it, magic casements); the sea is gently ruffled; in the middle distance is a boat, quietly rowing towards the castle; in the foreground is the placidly contemplative figure of a woman, and several equally placid deer. Any scene less perilous it would be hard to imagine. And we know precisely what impression it produced on Keats from his letter to Reynolds.[20]

> You know the Enchanted Castle, it doth stand
> Upon a Rock, on the Border of a Lake
> Nested in Trees, which all do seem to shake
> From some old Magic like Urganda's Sword.
> O Phoebus that I had thy sacred word
> To shew this Castle in fair dreaming wise
> Unto my friend, while sick and ill he lies.
>   You know it well enough, where it doth seem
> A mossy place, a Merlin's Hall, a dream.
> You know the clear Lake, and the little Isles,
>
> . . . .
>
>   The doors all look as if they op'd themselves,
> The windows as if latch'd by Fays and Elves –
>
> . . . .
>
>   See, what is coming from the distance dim!
> A golden galley all in silken trim!

There no doubt is the magic; but there, equally no doubt, are not the perilous seas. The verbal picture is just that of the original, a picture of dreaming peace. Here is another description, from a writer whose works elsewhere are full of casements, and of casements opening on the sea;[21] 'a room, the windows of which looked upon the sea. The wind burst in sudden squalls over the deep, and dashed the foaming waves against the rocks with inconceivable fury. The spray, notwithstanding the high situation of the castle, flew up with violence against the windows.... The moon shone faintly by intervals, through broken clouds upon the waters, illuming the white foam which burst around.'[22] That, whether we like it or not, is Mrs Radcliffe; and if we transport Claude's castle with its atmosphere of magic to the setting of Mrs Radcliffe's castle of Athlin, we have the picture complete. What we have not is the magic of the presentation, which is Keats' alone.

I do not believe that any reader who has watched Keats at work on the more exquisitely finished of the stanzas in 'The Eve of St Agnes', and seen this craftsman slowly elaborating and refining, will ever believe that this perfect stanza was achieved with the easy fluency with which, in the draft we have, it was obviously written down. All we can here see is the last two masterly touches.

Thou wast not born for death, immortal Bird
  No hungry generations tread thee down,
The voice I hear this passing night was heard
  In ancient days by Emperour and Clown
Perhaps the selfsame voicesong that found a path
Th[r]ough the sad heart of Ruth, when sick for home
She stood in tears amid the alien corn—
The same that oftimes hath
Cha[r]med the wide casements opening on the foam
Of

and then there was trouble over the epithet for *seas*, and trouble ever since for the decipherers of the first attempt. There stands after *Of* a heavily deleted word, of which the accepted reading has been *keelless*. But Mr Garrod is, and I have no doubt rightly, dubious about *keelless*. He says 'keelless' certainly does not correspond with the *ductus litterarum* – and I could wish that a good palaeographer should re-examine the MS.'[23]

I have no pretensions to being the good palaeographer that Mr Garrod (and I) would wish for. But I think it is clear that there were two stages of this word, not one, and that one of these was, or was going to be, *keelless*. Otherwise it is impossible to account for a vertical stroke at the beginning of the word, which is not part of the deletion, and even less part of the *r* that appears to be there. On the other hand, there is an unmistakable *t* before the loop of what has been taken to be the first *l* of *keelless*. What then was the word? Before we hurry into conjecture it may be as well to find out what the indefatigable Woodhouse thought about it. And it does not seem to have been observed that Woodhouse had no doubt what the cancelled word had been. He may have known from Keats himself, in which case his evidence is decisive; or he may have been merely making the best he could of it, in which case his reading has as much or as little authority as any one else's. But at least it should go on record. In his second book of transcripts there is a transcript of the poem in its final form, and in the margin Woodhouse has noted in his neat shorthand (Mavor's) all the important cancelled readings of the draft; and opposite this cancelled word he has written  , i.e. 'rthless' (presumably 'ruthless'. This does correspond with the *ductus litterarum*, with one small exception; it gives the required *t* and makes the loop the loop of the *h* of ruthless, not the *l* of *keelless*. I suggest that the sequence was first *keelless* perhaps not fully written out; then *ruthless*. But *ruthless* with its echo of the immediately preceding *Ruth* is clearly impossible; and the first synonym for it that occurs also suggests the sound of the far better word which then occurs to Keats and which he writes down, the last crowning touch to his stanza; and with the alteration of the rather insignificant *the wide*, we have the lines

Charm'd magic casements opening on the foam
Of perilous seas in fairy lands fo[r]lorn[24]

The last stanza is something of an anticlimax. The

poetic ecstasy is over and the poet comes back wearily to reality. Something of the same idea has occurred in *Endymion*, though in a different relation:

> There, where when wonders | ceas'd to float before,
> And thoughts of *self* came on, how crude and sore
> The journey homeward to *habitual self*!
> A mad-pursuing of the fog-born *elf*.
> Whose flitting lantern, through rude nettle-briar,
> *Cheats* us...... (ii 274)

and I am not sure that memories of the ubiquitous Mrs Radcliffe's *Romance of the Forest* are not traceable, memories of the phrases 'I fell into a sort of *walking dream*'[25] Is this a vision?',[26] 'not to mention the plantive accents of your voice'.[27]

> Fo[r]lorn! the very wor(l)d is like a bell

(his ear catches the coming alliteration too soon)

> To toll me back from thee unto myself
> Adieux! the fancy cannot cheat so well
> As she is fam'd to do, deceitfulving elf!
> Adieu! Adieu! thy plaintive Anthem fades
> Past the near meadows, over the still stream,
> Up the hill side, and now 'tis buried deep
> In the next vally's glades.
> Was it a vision real or waking dream?
> Fled is that Music – do I wake or sleep?

SOURCE: *Keats's Craftsmanship: A Study in Poetic Development* 1933; text from 1966 reprint.

NOTES

1. MBF, 63 (159).
2. I iii 164.
3. *End.* i 159.
4. Ibid. iv 767.
5. Ibid. ii 516.

6. MBF, 113 (315–16).
7. *End.* i 153–61; ii 511–17.
8. st. v 1 4.
9. E.g. the 'dance of the vintage' in *The Mysteries of Udolpho* (III p. 433): 'the festivity of the peasants. The scene was in a glade, where the trees, opening, formed a circle round the turf they highly overshadowed; between their branches, vines, loaded with ripe clusters, were hung in gay festoons; and beneath, were tables, with fruit, wine, cheese and other rural fare.... At a little distance, were benches for the elder peasants, few of whom, however, could forbear to join the jocund dance.'
10. *End.* iii 177.
11. There was clearly a pause in the writing after *them*; though this may have been due not to a need for reflection, but to a need for ink, since his pen appears to have run dry on the last stroke of *them*.
12. 'The sidelong view of swelling leafiness' ('Calidore', 34); 'Nymph of the downward smile and sidelong glance' (Sonnet to G.A.W., 1); sidelong aisles' (*End.* ii 264); 'sidelong laughing' (*End.* iv 211); 'sidelong fix'd her eye on Saturn's face' (*Hyp.* ii 91).
13. *The Mysteries of Udolpho,* I 178.
14. MBF, 130 (393).
15. Kipling, 'Wireless'.
16. MBF, 12 (19).
17. Ibid. 89 (261).
18. Ibid. 108 (309).
19. de S, 475; SC, 291 n., and more explicitly in a note to letter xlvi (in his edition).
20. MBF, 55 (135, 136).
21. E.g. 'the windows opened upon the sea' (SR, vol I, ch. ii, p. 60); 'Blanche withdrew to a window, the lower panes of which, being without painting, allowed her to observe the progress of the storm over the Mediterranean, whose dark waves, that had so lately slept, now came boldly swelling, in long succession, to the shore, where they burst in white foam' (*The Mysteries of Udolpho,* III 390).

22. AD, ch. ix, p. 185.
23. *Keats*, p. 117 n.
24. The reading *folorn* has exercised critics who wonder sadly whether Keats so pronounced the word. It is true enough that he more often than not wrote so (e.g. 'Eve of St Agnes', st. XXXVII, and 'Isabella', st. LXIII). But it is also true that *r* is the letter he is most careless about, and it is perpetually dropping out in his writing. So that we may suppose that Keats' pronunciation was better than his writing.
25. *Romance of the Forest*, vol. I, ch. iii, p. 66.
26. Ibid., vol. II, ch. ix, p. 56.
27. *The Mysteries of Udolpho*, I, 408 (ch. xiv, p. 76). and perhaps we may add to these, 'the nearer forest and the valley's stream' (*Romance of the Forest* I 208); and notice in comparison with stanza v the 'balmy sweets' and the 'wild musk-rose' of the sonnet on Sunrise in *The Romance of the Forest* (vol. III, ch. xvii, p. 145).

M. R. Ridley

THE ODES AND THE SONNET FORM (1933)

It is clear that, for whatever respective reasons, Keats was dissatisfied with both sonnet forms, and that his experiments, whether in single sonnets, or in an Ode which may be regarded as a loosely connected series of variously reformed sonnets, have not hitherto been very encouraging. The 'Fame' and 'Sleep' sonnets were awkward; the 'Ode to Psyche', having neither the free irregularity of the 'Pindaric' ode, nor the finished regularity of Keats' own Odes that are to follow, fell unhappily between two stools and gave an uneasy impression of trying to be recurrent and failing; while the 'Andromeda' sonnet, in a serious attempt to find out 'sandals more interwoven and complete', did little more than set the naked foot of poesy shuffling in ill-shapen and indeterminate carpet-slippers.

It looks as though from this time on Keats abandoned the sonnet as incorrigible; but he did not at all abandon his search for a verse form which should satisfy him, a stanza form which, while capable of that structural strength which comes from the correspondence of stanza with stanza, should yet avoid monotony, and should offer reasonable freedom of movement within the stanza. And this form, from the experience of his sonneteering experiments, he triumphantly created. All the four great Odes which follow that to Psyche have a stanza which consists of a Shakespearean quatrain followed by a Petrarchan sestet. The only variations are that in the 'Nightingale' Ode one line in the sestet is shortened, and that there is some diversity on the rhyme-scheme of the sestets. The 'Nightingale' Ode is the only one which holds steadily to one scheme throughout, the scheme being the straightforward *c d e c d e*; the 'Ode on Indolence' holds the same scheme for four stanzas, but in the fifth has *c d e d c e*, and in the last *c d e c e d* (one of the only two cases in the Odes in which the final rhyme is not the *e* rhyme); the 'Ode on Melancholy' holds it for two stanzas and then breaks in the last to *c d e d c e*; while the 'Ode on a Grecian Urn' cannot settle down to any one scheme; it has the *c d e d c e* in the first and last stanzas, and the unusual *c d e c e d* in the second.

The creation of this stanza was a noteworthy technical achievement. It gave Keats just what he wanted as a vehicle of expression, avoiding the defects which he felt in the two sonnet forms. In whichever form he found 'pouncing' rhymes he is rid of them, since he has discarded the Petrarchan octave and all but one of the Shakespearean quatrains; by the same stroke he is rid of the 'too elegiac' character; and he has discarded the final couplet. Let us set out one of the stanzas and examine its effect:

Who are these coming to the sacrifice?
  To what green altar, O mysterious priest,
Lead'st thou that heifer lowing at the skies,
  And all her silken flanks with garlands drest?
What little town by river or sea shore,
  Or mountain-built with peaceful citadel,
    Is emptied of this folk, this pious morn?
And, little town, thy streets for evermore
  Will silent be; and not a soul to tell
    Why thou art desolate, can e'er return.

There is no question about the first four lines; they have the neatness, concision and completeness which belong to any quatrain. But the effect of the remainder of the stanza is more subtle, and more interesting. If we are considering the stanza in isolation, and not as one of a series of a known form, we cannot tell when we reach the end of the sixth line whether we are merely in the middle of a second quatrain. But when we reach the end of the seventh line we get a very pleasant disappointment of the half-expectation with which we were rather uneasily awaiting the rhyme to the fifth line, and we get also a sense of space. We know that whatever happens there must be at least three more lines to come before the stanza can be rounded off, and our ear is led to expect the rounding off to be that of the sestet; and the expectation is pleasantly fulfilled. Here then is the stanza which Keats developed from the two sonnet forms; and we can observe with admiration how he contrives to make the best of both worlds. By shortening his stanza to ten lines, and employing the sestet, he gets rid at one stroke of the repetitive monotony of three successive quatrains and the over-clinching effect of the final couplet. On the other hand, in the Petrarchan sonnet the sestet tends to be overweighted by the octave, and the beauty of its rhyme-scheme tends to lose emphasis since it has too near a resemblance to the scheme of the octave. But in Keats' stanza the quatrain leads on to the fuller movement of the sestet, and the snap of the rhymes of the quatrain is a piquant contrast to and preparation for the slide of the rhymes of the sestet. And when we see the sestet thus more isolated than in the sonnet we become more aware of one of its peculiar beauties, the combined certainty and smoothness of the conclusion. The couplet jars to a halt with the brakes grinding; the sestet, with the foreseen second recurrence of the third rhyme, swings gently up into the wind and picks up its buoy.

This stanza Keats invented, and used in four of his six great Odes, with certain variations, all of them I think deliberate, and not accidental slips, in the rhyme-scheme of the sestet, and the shortening of one of the lines in each stanza of the 'Ode to a Nightingale'. When it has once been done, it looks, like many other notable inventions, obvious enough. How considerable a technical achievement it was we realize, I think, more clearly by seeing what happens when an inferior technician tries his hand at a somewhat similar experiment. For 'The Scholar Gipsy' and 'Thyrsis' Matthew Arnold adopted a stanza which also consists of quatrain and sestet, but both are Petrarchan, and the sestet precedes the quatrain. The result is a curiously invertebrate stanza. The sestet, in the first place, overweights the quatrain, much in the same way as the octave is apt to overweight the sestet in the full Petrarchan sonnet; and in the second place the rhyme-scheme of the Petrarchan quatrain unfits it for a conclusion. The stanzas do not come to an end which the ear expects and with which it is satisfied; they merely drift uneasily to a standstill. It looks as though Matthew Arnold became aware of the awkward balance between sestet and quatrain; but his remedy is worse than the disease. In fourteen of the twenty-five stanzas of 'The Scholar Gipsy', he has a heavier break at the end of the fifth line than at the end of the sixth. That is, in those stanzas he is not writing sestet-quatrain at all, but two quintets, rather feebly and awkwardly linked by the sixth line repeating the rhyme of the first. This stanza form has some merits; it has a certain easy and pensive fluency and from the very indecisiveness of the conclusion there is an easy slide from stanza to stanza. But it is a flaccid thing beside the firm and strongly articulated stanza of Keats. Here is an example of it:

Here, where the reaper was at work of late,
In this high field's dark corner, where he leaves
His coat, his basket, and his earthen cruise,
And in the sun all morning binds the sheaves,
Then here, at noon, comes back his stores to use;
Here will I sit and wait,
While to my ear from uplands far away
The bleating of the folded flocks is borne,
With distant cries of reapers in the corn –
All the live murmur of a summer's day.

SOURCE: *Keats's Craftmanship: A Study in Poetic Development*, 1933; text from 1966 reprint.

And here, to set against it, is Keats. Let us take the type that also has the shortened line, which Keats, with his sure instinct, uses where it is most telling, but which he evidently thought an unnecessary and restless variation, since he uses it only in the 'Nightingale' of the five 'regular' Odes.

Darkling I listen; and for many a time
  I have been half in love with easeful Death,
Called him soft names in many a mused rhyme,
  To take into the air my quiet breath;
Now more than ever seems it rich to die,
  To cease upon the midnight with no pain,
    While thou art pouring forth thy soul abroad
      In such an ecstasy!
  Still wouldst thou sing, and I have ears in vain—
    To thy high requiem become a sod.

One would have supposed that that stanza was achievement enough for any craftsman however exacting, for any critic of his own work however severe. But it did not satisfy Keats, and we find him four months later, in the poem 'To Autumn', adding the final touch which turned excellence into perfection. The firm opening quatrain is the same, with the strong break at the end of it. And we continue as before till the fifth line of the 'sestet' which now becomes a septet, since the sixth line, which we have learned to expect to conclude the stanza, does not give us the concluding rhyme, but rhymes with the fifth; and this slight disappointment of expectation, this slight suspense which is created by a couplet which we know cannot be the conclusion, leads us with an even more complete satisfaction, like that at the resolution of a discord, to the serene finality of the concluding rhyme.

Who hath not seen thee oft amid thy store?
  Sometimes whoever seeks abroad may find
Thee sitting careless on a granary floor,
  Thy hair soft-lifted by the winnowing wind;
Or on a half-reap'd farrow sound asleep,

Drows'd with the fame of poppies, while thy book
  Shares the next swath and all its twined flowers;
And sometimes like a gleaner thou dost keep
 Steady thy laden head across a brook;
 Or by a cyder-press, with patient look,
 Thou watchest the last oozings hours by hours.

SOURCE: as above.

Kenneth Burke

SYMBOLIC ACTION IN A POEM BY KEATS (1945)

We are here set to analyze the 'Ode on a Grecian Urn' as a viaticum that leads, by a series of transformations into the oracle, 'Beauty is truth, truth beauty'. We shall analyze the Ode 'dramatistically', in terms of symbolic action.

To consider language as means of *information* or *knowledge* is to consider it epistemologically, semantically, in terms of 'science'. To consider it as a mode of *action* is to consider it in terms of 'poetry'. For a poem is an act, the symbolic act of the poet who made it – an act of such a nature that, in surviving as a structure or object, it enables us as readers to re-enact it.

'Truth' being the essential word of knowledge (science) and 'beauty' being the essential word of art or poetry, we might substitute accordingly. The oracle would then assert, 'Poetry is science, science is poetry'. It would be particularly exhilarating to proclaim them one if there were a strong suspicion that they were at odds (as the assertion that 'God's in his heaven, all's right with the world' it is really a *counter*-assertion to doubts about God's existence and suspicions that much is wrong). It was the dialectical opposition between the 'esthetic' and the 'practical', with 'poetry' on one side and utility (business and applied science) on the other that was being ecstatically denied. The *relief* in this denial was grounded in the romantic philosophy itself, a philosophy which gave strong recognition to precisely the contrast between '*beauty*' and 'truth'.

Perhaps we might put it this way: If the oracle were to have been uttered in the first stanza of the poem rather than the last, its phrasing proper to that place would have been: Beauty is *not* truth, truth *not* beauty'. The five stanzas of successive transformation were necessary for the romantic philosophy of a romantic poet to transcend itself (raising its romanticism to a new order, or new dimension). An abolishing of romanticism through romanticism! (To transcend romanticism through romanticism is, when all is over, to restore in one way what is removed in another.)

But to the poem, step by step through the five stanzas.

As a 'way in', we begin with the sweeping periodic sentence that, before the stanza is over, has swiftly but imperceptibly been transmuted in quality from the periodic to the breathless, a cross between interrogation and exclamation:

Thou still unravish'd bride of quietness,
  Thou foster-child of silence and slow time,
Sylvan historian, who canst thus express
  A flowery tale more sweetly than our rhyme:
What leaf-fring'd legend haunts about thy shape
  Of deities or mortals, or of both,
    In Tempe or the dales of Arcady?
What men or gods are these? What maidens loth?
  What mad pursuit? What struggle to escape?
    What pipes and timbrels? What wild ecstasy?

Even the last quick outcries retain somewhat the quality of the periodic structure with which the stanza began. The final line introduces the subject of 'pipes and timbrels', which is developed and then surpassed in Stanza II:

Heard melodies are sweet, but those unheard
  Are sweeter; therefore, ye soft pipes, play on;
Not to the sensual ear, but, more endear'd,
  Pipe to the spirit ditties of no tone:

Fair youth, beneath the trees, thou canst not leave
Thy song, nor ever can those trees be bare;
Bold Lover, never, never canst thou kiss,
Though winning near the goal – yet, do not grieve;
She cannot fade, though thou hast not thy bliss,
Forever wilt thou love, and she be fair!

If we had only the first stanza of this Ode, and were speculating upon it from the standpoint of motivation, we could detect there tentative indication of two motivational levels. For the lines express a doubt whether the figures on the urn are 'deities or mortals' – and the motives of gods are of a different order from the motives of men. This bare hint of such a possibility emerges with something of certainty in the second stanza's development of the 'pipes and timbrels' theme. For we explicitly consider a contrast between body and mind (in the contrast between 'heard melodies', addressed 'to the sensual ear', and 'ditties of no tone', addressed 'to the spirit').

Also, of course, the notion of inaudible sound brings us into the region of the mystic oxymoron (the term in rhetoric for 'the figure in which an epithet of a contrary significance is added to a word: e.g., *cruel kindness*; *laborious idleness*'). And it clearly suggests a concern with the level of motives-behind-motives, as with the paradox of the prime mover that is itself at rest, being the unmoved ground of all motion and action. Here the poet whose sounds are the richest in our language is meditating upon *absolute* sound, the *essence* of sound, which would be soundless as the prime mover is motionless, or as the 'principle' of sweetness would not be sweet, having transcended sweetness, or as the sub-atomic particles of the sun are each, in their isolate purity, said to be devoid of temperature.

Contrast Keats's unheard melodies with those of Shelley:

Music, when soft voices die,

Vibrates in the memory—
Odours, when sweet violets sicken,
Live within the sense they quicken.

Rose leaves, when the rose is dead,
Are heaped for the beloved's bed;
And so thy thoughts, when thou art gone,
Love itself shall slumber on.

Here the futuristic Shelley is anticipating retrospection; he is looking forward to looking back. The form of thought is naturalistic and temporalistic in terms of *past* and *future*. But the form of thought in Keats is mystical, in terms of an *eternal present*. The Ode is striving to move beyond the region of becoming into the realm of *being*. (This is another way of saying that we are here concerned with two levels of motivation.)

In the last four lines of the second stanza, the state of immediacy is conveyed by a development peculiarly Keatsian. I refer not simply to translation into terms of the erotic, but rather to a quality of *suspension* in the erotic imagery, defining an eternal prolongation of the state just prior to fulfilment – not exactly arrested ecstasy, but rather an arrested pre-ecstasy.[1]

Suppose that we had but this one poem by Keats, and knew nothing of its author or its period, so that we could treat it only in itself, as a series of internal transformations to be studied in their development from a certain point, and without reference to any motives outside the Ode. Under such conditions, I think, we should require no further observations to characterize (from the standpoint of symbolic action) the main argument in the second stanza. We might go on to make an infinity of observations about the details of the stanza; but as regards major deployments we should deem it enough to note that the theme of 'pipes and timbrels' is developed by the use of mystic oxymoron, and then surpassed (or given a development-atop-the-development) by the stressing of erotic imagery (that had been ambiguously adumbrated in the references to 'maidens loth' and 'mad pursuit' of Stanza I). And we could note the quality of *incipience* in this imagery, its state of arrest not at fulfilment, but at the point just prior to fulfilment.

Add, now, our knowledge of the poem's place as an enactment in a particular cultural scene, and we likewise note in this second stanza a variant of the identification between death and sexual love that was so typical of 19th-century romanticism and was to attain its musical monument in the Wagnerian *Liebestod.* On a purely dialectical basis, to die in love would be to be born to love (the lovers dying as individual identities that they might be transformed into a common identity). Adding historical factors, one can note the part that capitalist individualism plays in sharpening this consummation (since a property structure that heightens the sense of individual identity would thus make it more imperiously a 'death' for the individual to take on the new identity made by a union of two). We can thus see why the love-death equation would be particularly representative of a romanticism that was the reflex of business.

Fortunately, the relation between private property and the love-death equation is attested on unimpeachable authority, concerning the effect of consumption and consummation in a 'mutual flame'.

> So between them love did shine,
> That the turtle saw his right
> Flaming in the phoenix' sight;
> Either was the other's mine.
>
> Property was thus appall'd,
> That the self was not the same;
> Single nature's double name
> Neither two nor one was called.

The addition of fire to the equation, with its pun on sexual burning, moves us from purely dialectical considerations into psychological ones. In the lines of Shakespeare, fire is the third term, the ground term for the other two (the synthesis that ends the lovers' roles as thesis and antithesis). Less obviously, the same movement from the purely dialectical to the psychological is implicit in any imagery of a *dying* or a *falling* in common, which when woven with sexual imagery signalizes a 'transcendent' sexual consummation. The figure appears in a lover's compliment when Keats writes to Fanny Brawne, thus:

> I never knew before, what such a love as you have made me feel, was; I did not believe in it; my Fancy was afraid of it lest it should burn me up. But if you will fully love me, though there may be some fire, 'twill not be more than we can bear when moistened and bedewed with pleasures.

Our primary concern is to follow the transformations of the poem itself. But to understand its full nature as a symbolic act, we should use whatever knowledge is available. In the case of Keats, not only do we know the place of this poem in his work and its time, but also we have material to guide our speculations as regards correlations between poem and poet. I grant that such speculations interfere with the symmetry of criticism as a game. (Criticism as a game is best to watch, I guess, when one confines himself to the single unit, and reports on its movements like a radio commentator broadcasting the blow-by-blow description of a prizefight.) But linguistic analysis has opened up new possibilities in the correlating of producer and product – and these concerns have such important bearing upon matters of culture and conduct in general that no sheer conventions or ideals of criticism should be allowed to interfere with their development.

From what we know of Keats's illness, with the peculiar inclination to erotic imaginings that accompany its fever (as with the writings of D. H. Lawrence) we can glimpse a particular bodily motive expanding and intensifying the lyric state in Keats's case. Whatever the intense *activity* of his thoughts, there was the material *pathos* of his physical condition. Whatever transformations of mind or body he experienced, his illness was there as a kind of constitutional substrate, whereby all aspects of the illness would be imbued with their derivation from a common ground (the phthisic fever thus being at one with the phthisic chill, for whatever the clear contrast between fever and chill, they are but modes of the same illness, the common underlying substance).

The correlation between the state of agitation in the poems and the physical condition of the poet is made quite clear in the poignant letters Keats wrote during his last illness. In 1819 he complains that he is 'scarcely content to write the best verses for the fever they leave behind'. And he continues: 'I want to compose without this fever'. But a few months later he confesses, 'I am recommended not even to read poetry, much less write it'. Or 'I must say that for 6 Months before I was taken ill I had not passed a tranquil day. Either that gloom overspre[a]d me or I was suffering under some passionate feeling, or if I turn'd to versify that exacerbated the poison of either sensation.' Keats was 'like a sick eagle looking at the sky', as he wrote of his mortality in a kindred poem, 'On Seeing the Elgin Marbles'.

But though the poet's body was a *patient*, the poet's mind was an *agent*. Thus, as a practitioner of poetry, he could *use* his fever, even perhaps encouraging, though not deliberately, esthetic habits that, in making for the perfection of his lines, would exact payment in the ravages of his body (somewhat as Hart Crane could write poetry only by modes of living that made for the cessation of his poetry and so led to his dissolution).

Speaking of agents, patients, and action here, we might pause to glance back over the centuries thus: in the Aristotelian grammar of motives, action has its reciprocal in passion, hence *passion* is the property of a *patient*. But by the Christian paradox (which made the martyr's action identical with his passion, as the accounts of the martyrs were called both Acts and Passionals), *patience* is the property of a moral *agent*. And this Christian view, as secularized in the philosophy of romanticism, with its stress upon creativeness, leads us to the possibility of a bodily suffering redeemed by a poetic act.

In the third stanza, the central stanza of the Ode (hence properly the fulcrum of its swing) we see the two motives, the action and the passion, in the process of being separated. The possibility raised in the first stanza (which was dubious whether the level of motives was to be human or divine), and developed in the second stanza (which contrasts the 'sensual' and the 'spirit'), becomes definitive in Stanza III:

Ah, happy, happy boughs! that cannot shed
  Your leaves, nor ever bid the Spring adieu;
And, happy melodist, unwearied,
  For ever piping songs for ever new;
More happy love! more happy, happy love!
  For ever warm and still to be enjoy'd,
    For ever panting, and for ever young;
All breathing human passion far above,
  That leaves a heart a high-sorrowful and cloy'd,
    A burning forehead, and a parching tongue.

The poem as a whole makes permanent, or fixes in a state of arrest, a peculiar agitation. But within this fixity, by the nature of poetry as a progressive medium, there must be development. Hence, the agitation that is maintained throughout (as a mood absolutized so that it fills the entire universe of discourse) will at the same time undergo internal transformations. In the third stanza, these are manifested as a clear division into two distinct and contrasted realms. There is a transcendental fever, which is felicitous, divinely above 'all breathing human passion'. And this 'leaves' the other level, the level of earthly fever, 'a burning forehead and a parching tongue'. From the bodily fever, which is a passion, and malign, there has split off a spiritual activity, a wholly benign aspect of the total agitation.

Clearly, a movement has been finished. The poem must, if it is well-formed, take a new direction, growing out of and surpassing the curve that has by now been clearly established by the successive stages from 'Is there the possibility of two motivational levels?' through 'there are two motivational levels' to 'the "active" motivational level "leaves" the "passive" level'.

Prophesying, with the inestimable advantage that goes with having looked ahead, what should we expect the new direction to be? First, let us survey the situation. Originally, before the two strands of the fever had been definitely drawn apart, the bodily passion could serve as the scene or ground of the spiritual action. But at the end of the third stanza, we abandon the level of bodily passion. The action is 'far above' the passion, it 'leaves' the fever. What then would this transcendent act require, to complete it?

It would require a scene of the same quality as itself. An act and a scene belong together. The nature of the one must be a fit with the nature of the other. (I like to call this the 'scene–act ratio', or 'dramatic ratio'.) Hence, the act having now transcended its bodily setting, it will require, as its new setting, a transcendent scene. Hence, prophesying *post eventum*, we should ask that, in Stanza IV, the poem *embody* the transcendental act by endowing it with an appropriate scene.

The scene–act ratio involves a law of dramatic consistency whereby the quality of the act shares the quality of the scene in which it is enacted (the synecdochic relation of container and thing contained). Its grandest variant was in supernatural cosmogonies wherein mankind took on the attributes of gods by acting in cosmic scenes that were themselves imbued with the presence of godhead.[2]

Or we may discern the logic of the scene–act ratio

behind the old controversy as to whether 'God willed the good because it is good', or 'the good is good because God willed it'. This strictly theological controversy had political implications. But our primary concern here is with the *dramatistic* aspects of this controversy. For you will note that the whole issue centers in the problems of the *grounds* of God's creative art.

Since, from the purely dramatic point of view, every act requires a scene in which it takes place, we may note that one of the doctrines (that 'God willed the good because it is good') is more symmetrical than the other. For by it, God's initial act of creation is itself given a ground, or scene (the objective existence of goodness, which was so real that God himself did not simply make it up, but acted in conformity with its nature when willing it to be the law of his creation). In the scholastic formulas taken over from Aristotle, God was defined as 'pure act' (though this pure act was in turn the ultimate ground or *scene* of human acting and willing). And from the standpoint of purely dramatic symmetry, it would be desirable to have some kind of 'scene' even for God. This requirement is met, we are suggesting, in the doctrine that 'God willed the good *because* it is good'. For this word, 'because', in assigning a reason for God's willing, gives us in principle a kind of scene, as we may discern in the pun of our word, 'ground', itself, which indeterminately applies to either 'place' or 'cause'.

If even theology thus responded to the pressure for dramatic symmetry by endowing God, as the transcendent act, with a transcendent scene of like quality, we should certainly expect to find analogous tactics in this Ode. For as we have noted that the romantic passion is the secular equivalent of the Christian passion, so we may recall Coleridge's notion that poetic action itself is a 'dim analogue of Creation'. Keats in his way confronting the same dramatistic requirement that the theologians confronted in theirs, when he has arrived at his transcendent act at the end of Stanza III (that is, when the benign fever has split away from the malign bodily counterpart, as a divorcing of spiritual action from sensual passion), he is ready in the next stanza for the imagining of a scene that would correspond in quality to the quality of the action as so transformed. His fourth stanza will concretize, or 'materialize', the act, by dwelling upon its appropriate ground.

> Who are these coming to the sacrifice?
> To what green altar, O mysterious priest,
> Lead'st thou that heifer lowing at the skies,
> And all her silken flanks with garlands drest?
> What little town, by river or sea shore,
> Or mountain built with peaceful citadel,
> Is emptied of this folk, this pious morn?
> And, little town, thy streets for evermore
> Will silent be; and not a soul to tell
> Why thou art desolate, can e'er return.

It is a vision, as you prefer, of 'death' or of 'immortality'. 'Immortality,' we might say, is the 'good' word for 'death', and must necessarily be conceived in terms of death (the necessity that Donne touches upon when he writes, '... but I thinke that I/Am, by being dead, immortall'). This is why, when discussing the second stanza, I felt justified in speaking of the variations of the love-death equation, though the poem spoke not of love and *death*, but of love *for ever*. We have a deathly-deathless scene as the corresponding ground of our transcendent act. The Urn itself, as with the scene upon it, is not merely an immortal act in our present mortal scene; it was originally an immortal act in a mortal scene quite different. The imagery, of sacrifice, piety, silence, desolation, is that of communication with the immortal or the dead.[3]

Incidentally, we might note that the return to the use of rhetorical questions in the fourth stanza serves well, on a purely technical level, to keep our contact with the mood of the opening stanza, a music that now but vibrates in the memory. Indeed, one even gets the impression that the form of the rhetorical question had never been abandoned; that the poet's questings had been couched as questions throughout. This is tonal felicity at its best, and something much like unheard tonal felicity. For the actual persistence of the rhetorical questions through these stanzas would have been wearisome, whereas their return now gives us an inaudible variation, by making us feel that the exclamations in the second and third stanzas had been questions, as the questions in the first stanza had been exclamations.

But though a lyric greatly profits by so strong a sense of continuousness, or perpetuity, I am trying to stress the fact that in the fourth stanza we *come upon* something. Indeed, this fourth stanza is related to the three foregoing stanzas quite as the sestet is related to the octave in Keats's sonnet, 'On First Looking Into Chapman's Homer':

Much have I travell'd in the realms of gold,
  And many goodly states and kingdoms seen;
  Round many western islands have I been
Which bards in fealty to Apollo hold.
Oft of one wide expanse had I been told
  That deep-brow'd Homer ruled as his demesne;
  Yet did I never breathe its pure serene
Till I heard Chapman speak out loud and bold;

Then felt I like some watcher of the skies
  When a new planet swims into his ken;
Or like stout Cortez when with eagle eyes
  He stared at the Pacific – and all his men
Look'd at each other with a wild surmise –
  Silent, upon a peak in Darien.

I am suggesting that, just as the sestet in this sonnet, *comes upon a scene,* so it is with the fourth stanza of the Ode. In both likewise we end on the theme of silence; and is not the Ode's reference to the thing that 'not a soul can tell' quite the same in quality as the sonnet's reference to a 'wild surmise'?

Thus, with the Urn as viaticum (or rather, with the *poem* as viaticum, and *in the name* of the Urn), having symbolically enacted a kind of act that transcends our mortality, we round out the process by coming to dwell upon the transcendental ground of this act. The dead world of ancient Greece, as immortalized on an Urn surviving from that period, is the vessel of this deathly – deathless ambiguity. And we have gone dialectically from the 'human' to the 'divine' and thence to the 'ground of the divine' (here tracing in poetic imagery the kind of 'dramatistic' course we have considered, on the purely conceptual plane, in the theological speculations about the 'grounds' for God's creative act). Necessarily, there must be certain inadequacies in the conception of this ground, precisely because of the fact that immortality can only be conceived in terms of death. Hence the reference to the 'desolate' in a scene otherwise possessing the benignity of the eternal.

The imagery of pious sacrifice, besides its fitness for such thoughts of departure as when the spiritual act splits from the sensual pathos, suggests also a bond of communication between the levels (because of its immortal character in a mortal scene). And finally, the poem, in the name of the Urn, or under the aegis of the Urn, is such a bond. For we readers, by re-enacting it in the reading, use it as a viaticum to transport us into the quality of the scene which it depicts on its face (the scene containing as a fixity what the poem as act extends into a process). The scene *on* the Urn is really the scene *behind* the Urn; the Urn is literally the ground of this scene, but transcendentally the scene is the ground of the Urn. The Urn contains the scene out of which it arose.

We turn now to the closing stanza:

O Attic shape! Fair attitude! with brede
  Of marble men and maidens overwrought,
With forest branches and the trodden weed;

Thou, silent form, dost tease us out of thought
As doth eternity: Cold Pastoral!
When old age shall this generation waste,
Thou shalt remain, in midst of other woe
Than ours, a friend to man, to whom thou say'st,
'Beauty is truth, truth beauty' – that is all
Ye know on earth, and all ye need to know.

In the third stanza we were at a moment of heat, emphatically sharing an imagery of loves 'panting' and 'for ever warm' that was, in the transcendental order, companionate to 'a burning forehead, and a parching tongue' in the order of the passions. But in the last stanza, as signalized in the marmorean utterance, 'Cold Pastoral!' we have gone from transcendental fever to transcendental chill. Perhaps, were we to complete our exegesis, we should need reference to some physical step from phthisic fever to phthisic chill, that we might detect here a final correlation between bodily passion and mental action. In any event we may note that, the mental action having departed from the bodily passion, the change from fever to chill is not a sufferance. For, as only the *benign* aspects of the fever had been left after the split, so it is a wholly benign chill on which the poem ends.[4]

I wonder whether anyone can read the reference to 'brede of marble men and maidens overwrought' without thinking of 'breed' for 'brede' and 'excited' for 'overwrought'. (Both expressions would thus merge notions of sexuality and craftsmanship, the erotic and the poetic.) As for the designating of the Urn as an 'Attitude', it fits in admirably with our stress upon symbolic action. For an attitude is an arrested, or incipient *act* – not just an *object*, or *thing*.

Yeats, in *A Vision*, speaks of 'the diagrams in Law's *Boehme*, where one lifts a paper to discover both the human entrails and the starry heavens'. This equating of the deeply without and the deeply within (as also with Kant's famous remark) might well be remembered when we think of the sky that the 'watcher' saw in Keats's sonnet. It is an internal sky, attained through meditations induced by the reading of a book. And so the oracle, whereby truth and beauty are proclaimed as one, would seem to derive from a profound inwardness.

Otherwise, without these introductory mysteries, 'truth' and 'beauty' were at odds. For whereas 'beauty' had its fulfilment in romantic poetry, 'truth' was coming to have its fulfilment in science, technological accuracy, accountancy, statistics, actuarial tables, and the like. Hence, without benefit of the rites which one enacts in a sympathetic reading of the Ode (rites that remove the discussion to a different level), the enjoyment of 'beauty' would involve an esthetic kind of awareness radically in conflict with the kind of awareness deriving from the practical 'truth'. And as regards the tactics of the poem, this conflict would seem to be solved by 'estheticizing' the true rather than by 'verifying' the beautiful.

Earlier in our essay, we suggested reading 'poetry' for 'beauty' and 'science' for 'truth', with the oracle deriving its *liberating* quality from the fact that it is uttered at a time when the poem has taken us to a level where earthly contradictions do not operate. But we might also, in purely conceptual terms, attain a level where 'poetry' and 'science' cease to be at odds; namely: by translating the two terms into the 'grammar' that lies behind them. That is: we could generalize the term 'poetry' by widening it to the point where we could substitute for it the term 'act'. And we could widen 'science' to the point where we could substitute 'scene'. Thus we have:

'beauty'	equals	'poetry'	equals	'act'
'truth'	equals	'science'	equals	'scene'

We would equate 'beauty' with 'act', because it is not merely a decorative thing, but an assertion, an affirmative, a creation, hence in the fullest sense an act. And we would equate 'truth' or 'science' with the 'scenic' because science is a knowledge of *what is* – and *all that is* comprises the over-all universal *scene*. Our corresponding transcendence, then, got by 'translation' into purely grammatical terms, would be: 'Act is scene, scene act'. We have got to this point by a kind of purely conceptual transformation that would correspond, I think, to the transformations of imagery leading to the oracle in the Ode.

'Act is scene, scene act.' Unfortunately, I must break the symmetry a little. For poetry, as conceived in idealism (romanticism), could not quite be equated with *act*, but rather with *attitude*. For idealistic philosophies, with their stress upon the subjective, place primary stress upon the *agent* (the individual, the ego, the will, etc.). It was medieval scholasticism that placed primary stress upon the *act*. And in the Ode the Urn (which is the vessel or representative of poetry) is called an 'attitude', which is not outright an act, but an incipient or arrested act, a *state of mind*, the property of an *agent*. Keats, in calling the Urn an attitude, is *personifying* it. Or we might use the italicizing resources of dialectic by saying that for Keats, beauty (poetry) was not so much 'the *act* of an agent' as it was 'the act of an *agent*'.

Perhaps we can re-enforce this interpretation by examining kindred strategies in Yeats, whose poetry similarly derives from idealistic, romantic sources. Indeed, as we have noted elsewhere,[5] Yeats's vision of immortality in his Byzantium poems but carries one step further the Keatsian identification with the Grecian Urn:

> Once out of nature I shall never take
> My bodily form from any natural thing,
> But such a form as Grecian goldsmiths make
> Of hammered gold and gold enamelling ...'

Here certainly the poet envisions immortality as 'esthetically' as Keats. For he will have immortality as a golden bird, a fabricated thing, a work of Grecian goldsmiths. Here we go in the same direction as the 'overwrought' Urn, but farther along in that direction.

The ending of Yeats's poem, 'Among School Children', helps us to make still clearer the idealistic stress upon agent:

> Labour is blossoming or dancing where
> The body is not bruised to pleasure soul,
> Nor beauty born out of its own despair,
> Nor blear-eyed wisdom out of midnight oil.
> O chestnut tree, great rooted blossomer,
> Are you the leaf, the blossom or the bole?
> O body swayed to music, O brightening glance,
> How can we know the dancer from the dance?

Here the chestnut tree (as personified agent) is the ground of unity or continuity for all its scenic manifestations; and with the agent (dancer) is merged the act (dance). True, we seem to have here a commingling of act, scene, and agent, all three. Yet it is the *agent* that is 'foremost among the equals'. Both Yeats and Keats, of course, were much more 'dramatistic' in their thinking than romantic poets generally, who usually center their efforts upon the translation of *scene* into terms of *agent* (as the materialistic science that was the dialectical counterpart of romantic idealism preferred conversely to translate *agent* into terms of *scene*, or in other words, to treat 'consciousness' in terms of 'matter', the 'mental' in terms of the 'physical', 'people' in terms of 'environment').

To review briefly: The poem begins with an ambiguous fever which in the course of the further development is 'separated out', splitting into a bodily fever and a spiritual counterpart. The bodily passion is the malign aspect of the fever, the mental action its benign aspect. In the course of the development, the malign passion is transcended and the benign active partner, the intellectual exhilaration, takes over. At the beginning, where the two aspects were ambiguously one, the bodily passion would be the 'scene' of the mental action (the 'objective symptoms' of the body would be paralleled by the 'subjective symptoms' of the mind, the bodily state thus being the other or ground of the mental state). But as the two become separated out, the mental action transcends the bodily passion. It becomes an act in its own right, making discoveries and assertions not grounded in the bodily passion. And this quality of action, in transcending the merely physical symptoms of the fever, would thus require a different ground or scene, one more suited in quality to the quality of the transcendent act.

The transcendent act is concretized, or 'materialized', in the vision of the 'immortal' scene, the reference in Stanza IV to the original scene of the Urn, the 'heavenly' scene of a dead, or immortal, Greece (the scene in which the Urn was originally enacted and which is also fixed on its face). To indicate the internality of this vision, we referred to a passage in Yeats relating the 'depths' of the sky without to the depths of the mind within; and we showed a similar pattern in Keats's account of the vision that followed his reading of Chapman's Homer. We suggested that the poet is here coming upon a new internal sky, through identification with the Urn as act, the same sky that he came upon through identification with the enactments of Chapman's translation.

This transcendent scene is the level at which the earthly laws of contradiction no longer prevail. Hence, in the terms of this scene, he can proclaim the unity of truth and beauty (of science and art), a proclamation which he needs to make precisely because here was the basic split responsible for the romantic agitation (in both poetic and philosophic idealism). That is, it was gratifying to have the oracle proclaim the unity of poetry and science because the values of technology and business were causing them to be at odds. And from the perspective of a 'higher level' (the perspective of a dead or immortal scene transcending the world of temporal contradictions) the split could be proclaimed once more a unity.

At this point, at this stage of exaltation, the fever has been replaced by chill. But the bodily passion has completely dropped out of account. All is now mental action. Hence, the chill (as in the ecstatic exclamation, 'Cold Pastoral!') is proclaimed only in its benign aspect.

We may contrast this discussion with explanations such as a materialist of the Kretschmer school might offer. I refer to accounts of motivation that might treat disease as cause and poem as effect. In such accounts, the disease would not be 'passive', but wholly active; and what we have called the mental action would be wholly passive, hardly more than an epiphenomenon, a mere symptom of the disease quite as are the fever and the chill themselves. Such accounts would give us no conception of the essential matter here, the intense linguistic activity.

SOURCE: *A Grammar of Motives*, New York, 1945.

NOTES

1. Mr G. Wilson Knight, in *The Starlit Dome*, refers to 'that recurring tendency in Keats to image a poised form, a stillness suggesting motion, what might be called a "tiptoe" effect'.

2. In an article by Leo Spitzer, '*Milieu* and *Ambiance*: An Essay in Historical Semantics' (September and December 1942 numbers of *Philosophy and Phenomenological Research*), one will find a wealth of material that can be read as illustrative of 'dramatic ratio'.

3. In imagery there is no negation, or disjunction. Logically, we can say, 'this *or* that', 'this, *not* that'. In imagery we can but say 'this *and* that', 'this *with* that', 'this–that', etc. Thus, imagistically considered, a commandment cannot be simply a proscription, but is also latently a provocation (a state of affairs that figures in the kind of stylistic scrupulosity and/or curiosity

to which Glide's heroes have been particularly sensitive, as 'thou shalt not ...' becomes imaginatively transformed into 'what would happen if ...'). In the light of what we have said about the deathiness of immortality, and the relation between the erotic and the thought of a 'dying', perhaps we might be justified in reading the last line of the great 'Bright Star!' sonnet as naming states not simply alternative but also synonymous:

> And so live ever – or else swoon to death.

This use of the love–death equation is as startlingly paralleled in a letter to Fanny Brawne:

> I have two luxuries to brood over in my walks, your loveliness and the hour of my death. O that I could take possession of them both in the same moment.

4. In a letter to Fanny Brawne, Keats touches upon the fever–chill contrast in a passage that also touches upon the love–death equation, though here the chill figures in an untransfigured state:

> I fear that I am too prudent for a dying kind of Lover. Yet, there is a great difference between going off in warm blood like Romeo; and making one's exit like a frog in a frost.

5. 'On Motivation in Yeats', *Southern Review* (winter 1942).

BRIEF NOTES ON THE 'URN' PROBLEM

1.

It is usual, I believe, to take the concluding couplet of Keats's 'Ode to a Grecian Urn' as conveying the message of the Urn to mankind in general....

An alternative suggestion is to assume that the 'ye' of the last line is addressed to the figures on the Urn. For them Beauty *is* Truth because their experience is limited to the beautiful as depicted on the Urn. As Keats points out in the second and third stanzas, they would have none of the drawbacks of the ordinary course of experience. The Urn's message, if addressed to the world in general, and if literally interpreted, is absurd; but the Urn remains 'a friend to man' because when he contemplates it he can escape from the real world to the world of the imagination, where Beauty *is* Truth. This interpretation, of course, requires that only the words 'Beauty is Truth, Truth Beauty' be printed in inverted commas, as in Professor de Selincourt's edition.

SOURCE: G. St Quintin, 'The Grecian Urn', *The Times Literary Supplement*, 5 February 1938.

2.

The message of the Grecian Urn has, unhappily, more often teased critics out of thought than into it. This very brief study ... seeks ... by a careful study of the original texts to discover just how the famous apothegm of the urn fits into the poem. In doing so, we may discredit one or two older interpretations and show, at least, what the last lines of the ode cannot mean...

It is from the last stanza and particularly the last two lines that all our critical difficulties spring....

One troublesome question has been asked often enough but rarely answered with care: at the very end of the ode, who is saying what to whom? The first published version of the poem, in the *Annal of the Fine Arts*, early in 1820, read:

> Beauty is truth, truth beauty. – That is all
> Ye know on earth, and all ye need to know.[1]

The second appearance of the lines in print, in the *Lamia* volume of 1820, wore slightly different punctuation:

> 'Beauty is truth, truth beauty', – that is all
> Ye know on earth, and all ye need to know.

These readings give us three possible interpretations: either both lines are spoken by the urn, but the extra-sententiousness of the first five words merits special pointing; or the first five words are spoken by the urn, the rest by the poet to the reader; or the first five words are spoken by the urn, the rest by the poet to the figures he has just described.

The last contention [that of G. St Quintin, above] should die of natural incongruity. It is artistically as well as philosophically unthinkable that Keats should suddenly intrude himself in this way to tell the figures on the urn that they had grasped the one simple regimen of life and need know nothing else, that they were, indeed, probably better off in their pristine ignorance. Keats, to whom the world meant intensely, had no place in his philosophy for noble savages, even Greek ones.

The answer to the riddle of the proper reading, however, lies not in critical speculation but in textual analysis. The two original printings can claim no great authority. The *Annals* text was based on a copy begged of Keats by Haydon, who was not noted for his trustworthiness. As for the *Lamia* version, it is well known that Keats was too ill to oversee the publication of his

1820 volume which was, partially at least, edited by John Taylor.

One must fall back on the manuscripts. Unfortunately, no holograph is known to survive, but there are four transcripts, all unquestionably not far removed from the original, and all of them agree.

The transcript by George Keats (in the British Museum) reads:

> Beauty is truth, – Truth Beauty, – that is all
> Ye know on earth, and all ye need to know.

Charles Wentworth Dilke (in his copy of *Endymion*, in the Keats Memorial House, Hampstead):

> Beauty is truth, – truth beauty, – that is all
> Ye know on earth, and all ye need to know.

Charles Armitage Brown (Harvard Keats Collection):

> Beauty is Truth, – Truth Beauty, – that is all
> Ye know on earth, and all ye need to know.

Richard Woodhouse (Harvard):

> Beauty is Truth, – Truth beauty, – That is all
> Ye know on earth, and all ye need to know.

All four transcripts, then, not only lack the full stop and inverted commas of the *Annals* and *Lamia* texts respectively, but they have an additional dash between the two phrases, 'Beauty is truth' and 'truth beauty', thus breaking up the concluding lines of the poem into three rather than two parts. A threefold division must negate the possibility of a dual statement which depends on some mechanical indication ... of the complete integrity of the initial five-word phrase. The transcripts obviously infer a single statement uttered by the urn without any interference on the part of the poet. ... What the message of the urn may mean is, of course, another matter.

SOURCE: Alvin Whitley, 'The Message of the Grecian Urn', *Keats–Shelley Memorial Bulletin,* v (1953)

NOTE

1. [Editor's note.] An incorrect transcription. It should be,

> Beauty is Truth, Truth Beauty. – That is all
> Ye know on Earth, and all ye need to know.

3.

Turn now to Keats and you are returned upon *mere* poetry, in the Latin sense of *mere.*[1] Keats has no politics, no philosophy of statecraft, little social feeling: he is a young apostle of poetry for poetry's sake.

> Beauty is truth, truth beauty, – that is all
> Ye know on earth and all ye need to know.

But of course, to put it solidly, that is a vague observation – to anyone whom life has taught to face facts and define his terms, actually an *uneducated* conclusion, albeit most pardonable in one so young and ardent

SOURCE: Sir Arthur Quiller-Couch, *Charles Dickens and other Victorians,* New York, 1925.

NOTE

1. [Editor's note.] 'Pure', 'unmixed'.

4.

(*a*) The possibilities of human misunderstanding make up indeed a formidable subject for study, but something more can be done to elucidate it than has yet been attempted. Whatever else we may do by the light of nature, it would be folly to maintain that we should read by it....

But Feeling (and sometimes Tone) may take charge of and operate through Sense in another fashion, one more constantly relevant in poetry....

When this happens, the statements which appear in the poetry are there for the sake of their effects upon feelings, not for their own sake. Hence to challenge their truth or to question whether they deserve serious attention as *statements claiming truth*, is to mistake their function. The point is that many, if not most, of the statements in poetry are there *as a means* to the manipulation and expression of feelings and attitudes, not as contributions to any body of doctrine of any type whatever.... (W)ith philosophical or meditative poetry there is great danger of a confusion which may have two sets of consequences.

On the one hand there are very many people who, if they read any poetry at all, try to take all its statements seriously – and find them silly. On the other hand there are those who succeed too well, who swallow 'Beauty is Truth, truth beauty ...' as the quintessence of an aesthetic philosophy, not as the expression of a certain blend of feelings, and proceed into a complete stalemate of muddle-mindedness as a result of their linguistic naivety.

SOURCE: I. A. Richards, *Practical Criticism*, 1929.

(*b*) The reader will notice that a superfluity of meanings, not any lack of meaning, is the difficulty. The fact that the ranges of Beauty and Truth overlap at three points (B5=T2b; B8=T5; B9=T4b) gives to the equivalence, either as a gesture or as having some indefensible sense, a peculiarly strong suasive force. And this accounts for its power *in the poem* (when, of course, it is not apprehended analytically) to convey that feeling of deep acceptance which is often a chief phase in the aesthetic experience. The poem is perhaps unusual in having an aesthetic experience for *subject* as well as for aim.

SOURCE: I. A. Richards, *Mencius on the Mind,* 1923.

5.

And I confess to considerable difficulty in analysing my own feelings, a difficulty which makes me hesitate to accept Mr Richards's theory of 'pseudo-statements'. On reading the line which he uses,

Beauty is truth, truth beauty ...

I am at first inclined to agree with him, because this statement of equivalence means nothing to me. But on re-reading the whole Ode, this line strikes me as a serious blemish on a beautiful poem, and the reason must be either that I fail to understand it, or that it is a statement which is untrue. And I suppose that Keats meant something by it, however remote his truth and his beauty may have been from these words in ordinary use. And I am sure he would have repudiated any explanation of the line which called it a pseudo-statement. ... The statement of Keats seems to me meaningless; or perhaps the fact that it is grammatically meaningless conceals another meaning from me.

SOURCE: T. S. Eliot, *Dante,* 1929; reprinted in *Selected Essays,* 1932.

6.

The idea that the pursuit of beauty eats up the pursuer, who therefore sacrifices himself to it, is really not a remote one for a romantic poet. ... Beauty is both a cause of and an escape from suffering, and in either way suffering is deeply involved in its production. Here is the crisis of the poem; in the sudden exertion of muscle by which Keats skids round the corner from self-pity to an imaginative view of the world. None of these people can get anything out of the world except beauty, and at once we turn back to the poet with a painful ecstasy in the final stanza; there is nothing else left. This is the force behind the cry 'Beauty is Truth' (obviously, I think), however the terms of it are to be interpreted.

The chief puzzle about this is that one feels the poem has raised no question about truth before. ... This, I take it, was why Mr Middleton Murry defended the philosophy of the last three lines but doubted their value in the poem (thus taking a position precisely opposite to Professor Richards's). Such an objection would not occur to Mr Brooks, who takes it as doctrine that a lyrical poet is concerned with philosophical truth. Already in the first verse, he points out, the pot is called a historian, so is expected to tell truth, but its history has 'no footnotes' and is merely an imaginative insight; 'if we have followed the development of the metaphors ... we shall be prepared for the enigmatic final paradox' in which the urn 'speaks as a character in the drama and makes a commentary on its own nature.' This is sufficient for an answer to Mr Murry, I think. But we cannot suppose that the aphorism is merely dramatic, in the sense of being a suitable remark for a silent pot. ... If we were sure that Keats did not agree with the pot, the climax would become trivial. However little we are to use biography, it seems fair to quell this doubt by remembering that Keats had wrestled with the idea in prose. 'The excellence of every art is in its intensity, capable of making all disagreeables evaporate from their being in close relation to Beauty and Truth. ... What the imagination seizes as Beauty must be Truth,' and so on. That is, I take it, his mind was working on the ideas of Coleridge. But there is remarkably little agony in Coleridge's theory of Imagination (remarkably, I mean, for so unhappy a man); whereas Keats was trying to work the disagreeables into the theory. It seemed to him, therefore, that the aphorism was *somehow* relevant to the parching tongue, the desolate streets, and the other woes of the generations not yet wasted. He, like his readers, I think, was puzzled by the remarks of the pot, and yet felt that they were very *nearly* intelligible and relevant. It struck me that the philosophical approach of Mr Brooks gave a slightly wrong twist to:

> Thou, silent form, dost tease us out of thought
> As doth eternity. Cold pastoral!

'It is enigmatic as eternity is, for like eternity its history is outside time, beyond time, and for this very reason bewilders our time-ridden minds. It teases us.' It teases us *out of thought*; it stops us thinking; the idea is more suited to a mystical ecstasy than a metaphysical puzzle. And we have reached this condition through a 'sacrifice'; for that matter, the usual function of an urn is to hold the ashes of the dead. What it tells us is a revelation, and revelations are expected to be puzzling. In short, if we recognise the stress of feeling in the rest of the poem, I do not think a reasonable man would withhold his sympathy from the end of it ...

However, to say that all this was present for Keats, as a feeling that the pot had summed up a far-reaching mystery, does not say that the lines are good ones, and that the reader ought to feel it too. It often happens that a poet has built his machine, putting all the parts into it and so on very genuinely, and the machine does not go. I think that 'Oh Attic shape! Fair attitude! with brede' is a very bad line; the half pun suggesting a false Greek derivation and jammed against an arty bit of Old English seems to be affected and ugly; it is the sort of thing that the snobbish critics of his own time called him a Cockney for. One might feel, as Robert Bridges clearly did, that the last lines with their brash attempt to end with a smart bit of philosophy have not got enough knowledge behind them, and are flashy in the same way. I do not feel this myself, only that the effort of seeing the thing as Keats did is too great to be undertaken with pleasure. There is perhaps a great puzzle about how far we ought to make this kind of effort, and at what point the size of the effort required simply proves the poem to be bad. But in any case, I do not think the lines need to be regarded either as purely Emotive or a fully detached bit of philosophising.

SOURCE: William Empson, *The Structure of Complex Words,* 1931.

[Editor's note.] These extracts are all to be found in Harvey T. Lyon's *Keats' Well-Read Urn* (New York, 1958), though I have given a slightly fuller transcript of part of the Empson passage from *Complex Words.* The Brooks essay is printed in full elsewhere in this volume.

Cleanth Brooks

KEATS'S SYLVAN HISTORIAN (1944)

There is much in the poetry of Keats which suggests that he would have approved of Archibald MacLeish's dictum, 'A poem should not mean/But be.' There is even some warrant for thinking that the Grecian urn (real or imagined) which inspired the famous ode was, for Keats, just such a poem, 'palpable and mute', a poem in stone. Hence it is the more remarkable that the 'Ode' itself differs from Keats's other odes by culminating in a statement – a statement even of some sententiousness in which the urn itself is made to say that beauty is truth, and – more sententious still – that this bit of wisdom sums up the whole of mortal knowledge.

This is 'to mean' with a vengeance – to violate the doctrine of the objective correlative, not only by stating truths, but by defining the limits of truth. Small wonder that some critics have felt that the unravished bride of quietness protests too much.

T. S. Eliot, for example, says that 'this line ['Beauty is truth', etc.] strikes me as a serious blemish on a beautiful poem; and the reason must be either that I fail to understand it, or that it is a statement which is untrue.' But even for persons who feel that they do understand it, the line may still constitute a blemish. Middleton Murry, who, after a discussion of Keats's other poems and his letters, feels that he knows what Keats meant by 'beauty' and what he meant by 'truth', and that Keats used them in senses which allowed them to be properly bracketed together, still, is forced to conclude: 'My own opinion concerning the value of these two lines *in the context of the poem itself* is not very different from Mr T. S. Eliot's.' The troubling assertion is apparently an intrusion upon the poem –

does not grow out of it – is not dramatically accommodated to it.

This is essentially Garrod's objection, and the fact that Garrod does object that a distaste for the ending of the 'Ode' is by no means limited to critics of notoriously 'modern' sympathies.

But the question of real importance is not whether Eliot, Murry, and Garrod are right in thinking that 'Beauty is truth, truth beauty' injures the poem. The question of real importance concerns beauty and truth in a much more general way; what is the relation of the beauty (the goodness, the perfection) of a poem to the truth or falsity of what it seems to assert? It is a question which has particularly vexed our own generation – to give I. A. Richards's phrasing, it is the problem of belief.

The 'Ode', by its bold equation of beauty and truth, raises this question in its sharpest form – the more so when it becomes apparent that the poem itself is obviously intended to be a parable on the nature of poetry, and of art in general. The 'Ode' has apparently been an enigmatic parable, to be sure: one can emphasize *beauty* is truth and throw Keats into the pure-art camp, the usual procedure. But it is only fair to point out that one could stress *truth* is beauty, and argue with the Marxist critics of the 'thirties for a propaganda art. The very ambiguity of the statement, 'Beauty is truth, truth beauty' ought to warn us against insisting very much on the statement in isolation, and to drive us back to a consideration of the context in which the statement is set.

It will not be sufficient, however, if it merely drives us back to a study of Keats's reading, his conversation, his letters. We shall not find our answer there even if scholarship does prefer on principle investigations of Browning's ironic question, 'What porridge had John Keats?' For even if we knew just what porridge he had, physical and mental, we should still not be able to settle the problem of the 'Ode'. The reason should be clear: our specific question is not what did Keats the man perhaps want to assert here about the relation of beauty and truth: it is rather: was Keats the poet able to exemplify that relation in this particular poem? Middleton Murry is right: the relation of the final statement in the poem to the total context is all-important.

Indeed, Eliot, in the very passage in which he attacks the 'Ode' has indicated the general line which we are to take in its defence. In that passage, Eliot goes on to contrast the closing lines of the 'Ode' with a line from *King Lear*, 'Ripeness is all'. Keats's lines strike him as false; Shakespeare's, on the other hand, as not clearly false, and as possibly quite true. Shakespeare's generalization, in other words, avoids raising the question of truth. But is it really a question of truth and falsity? One is tempted to account for the difference of effect which Eliot feels in this way: 'Ripeness is all' is a statement put in the mouth of a dramatic character and a statement which is governed and qualified by the whole context of the play. It does not directly challenge an examination into its truth because its relevance is pointed up and modified by the dramatic context.

Now, suppose that one could show that Keats's lines, *in quite the same way*, constitute a speech, a consciously riddling paradox, put in the mouth of a particular character, and modified by the total context of the poem. If we could demonstrate that the speech was 'in character', was dramatically appropriate, was properly prepared for—then would not the lines have all the justification of 'Ripeness is all'? In such case, should we not have waived the question of the scientific or philosophic truth of the lines in favour of the application of a principle curiously like that of dramatic propriety? I suggest that some such principle is the only one legitimately to be invoked in any case. Be that as it may, the 'Ode on a Grecian Urn' provokes us with as neat an instance as one could wish in order to test the implications of such a manoeuvre.

It has seemed best to be perfectly frank about procedure: the poem is to be read in order to see whether the last lines of the poem are not, after all, dramatically prepared for. Yet there are some claims to be made upon the reader too, claims which he, for his part, will have to be prepared to honour. He must not be allowed to dismiss the early characterizations of the urn as merely so much vaguely beautiful description. He must not be too much surprised if 'mere decoration' turns out to be meaningful symbolism – or if ironies develop where he has been taught to expect only sensuous pictures. Most of all, if the teasing riddle spoken finally by the urn is not to strike him as a bewildering break in tone, he must not be too much disturbed to have the element of paradox latent in the poem emphasized, even in those parts of the poem which have none of the energetic crackle of wit with which he usually associates paradox. This is surely not too much to ask of the reader – namely, to assume that Keats meant what he said and that he chose his words with care. After all, the poem begins on a note of paradox, though a mild one: for we ordinarily do not expect an urn to speak at all; and yet, Keats does more than this: he begins his poem by emphasizing the apparent contradiction.

The silence of the urn is stressed—it is a 'bride of quietness'; it is a 'foster-child of silence', but the urn is a 'historian' too. Historians tell the truth, or are at least expected to tell the truth. What is a 'Sylvan historian'? A historian who is like the forest rustic, a woodlander? Or, a historian who writes histories of the forest? Presumably, the urn is sylvan in both senses. True, the latter meaning is uppermost: the urn can 'express/A flowery tale more sweetly than our rhyme', and what the urn goes on to express is a 'leaf-fring'd legend' of 'Tempe or the dales of Arcady'. But the urn, like the 'leaf-ring'd legend' which it tells, is covered with emblems of the fields and forests: 'Overwrought,/With forest branches and the trodden weed'. When we consider the way in which the urn utters its history, the fact that it must be sylvan in both senses is seen as inevitable. Perhaps too the fact that it is a rural historian, a rustic, a peasant historian, qualifies in our minds the dignity and the 'truth' of the histories which it recites. Its histories, Keats has already conceded, may be characterized as 'tales' – not formal history at all.

The sylvan historian certainly supplies no names and dates – 'What men or gods are these?' the poet asks. What it does give is action – of men *or* gods, of godlike men or of superhuman (though not daemonic) gods – action, which is not the less intense for all that the urn is cool marble. The words 'mad' and 'ecstasy' occur, but it is the quiet, rigid urn which gives the dynamic picture. And the paradox goes further: the scene is one of violent love-making, a Bacchanalian scene, but the urn itself is like a 'still unravish'd bride', or like a child, a child 'of silence and slow time'. It is not merely like a child, but like a 'foster-child'. The exactness of the term can be defended. 'Silence and slow time', it is suggested, are not the true parents, but foster-parents. They are too old, one feels, to have borne the child themselves. Moreover, they dote upon the 'child' as grandparents do. The urn is fresh and unblemished; it is still young, for all its antiquity, and time which destroys so much has 'fostered' it.

With Stanza II we move into the world presented by the urn, into an examination, not of the urn as a whole – as an entity with its own form – but of the details which overlay it. But as we enter that world, the paradox of silent speech is carried on, this time in terms of the objects portrayed on the vase.

The first lines of the stanza state a rather bold paradox – even the dulling effect of many readings has hardly blunted it. At least we can easily revive its sharpness. Attended to with care, it is a statement which is preposterous, and yet true – true on the same level on which the original metaphor of the speaking urn is true. The unheard music is sweeter than any audible music. The poet has rather cunningly enforced his conceit by using the phrase, 'ye soft pipes'. Actually, we might accept the poet's metaphor without being forced to accept the adjective 'soft'. The pipes might, although 'unheard', be shrill, just as the action which is frozen in the figures on the urn can be violent and ecstatic as in Stanza I and slow and dignified as in Stanza IV (the procession to the sacrifice). Yet, by characterizing the pipes as 'soft', the poet has provided a sort of realistic basis for his metaphor: the pipes, it is suggested, are playing very softly; if we listen carefully, we can hear them; their music is just below the threshold of normal sound.

This general paradox runs through the stanza: action goes on though the actors are motionless; the song will not cease; the lover cannot leave his song; the maiden, always to be kissed, never actually kissed, will remain changelessly beautiful. The maiden is, indeed, like the urn itself, a 'still unravished bride of quietness' – not even ravished by a kiss; and it is implied, perhaps, that her changeless beauty, like that of the urn, springs from this fact.

The poet is obviously stressing the fresh, unwearied charm of the scene itself which can defy time and is deathless. But, at the same time, the poet is being perfectly fair to the terms of his metaphor. The beauty portrayed is deathless because it is lifeless. And it would be possible to shift the tone easily and ever so slightly by insisting more heavily on some of the phrasings so as to give them a darker implication. Thus, in the case of 'thou canst not leave/Thy song', one could interpret: the musician cannot leave the song even if he would: he is fettered to it, a prisoner. In the same way, one could enlarge on the hint that the lover is not wholly satisfied and content: 'never canst thou kiss,/ ... *yet, do not grieve*'. These items are mentioned here, not because one wishes to maintain that the poet is bitterly ironical, but because it is important for us to see that even here the paradox is being used fairly, particularly in view of the shift in tone which comes in the next stanza.

This third stanza represents, as various critics have pointed out, a recapitulation of earlier motifs. The boughs which cannot shed their leaves, the unwearied melodist, and the ever-ardent lover reappear. Indeed, I am not sure that this stanza can altogether be defended against the charge that it represents a falling-off from the delicate but firm precision of the earlier stanzas. There is a tendency to linger over the scene sentimentally: the repetition of the word 'happy' is perhaps symptomatic of what is occurring. Here, if anywhere, in my opinion, is to be found the blemish on the ode – not in the last two lines. Yet, if we are to attempt a defence of the third stanza, we shall come nearest success by emphasizing the paradoxical implications of the repeated items; for whatever development there is in the stanza inheres in the increased stress on the paradoxical element. For example, the boughs cannot 'bid the Spring adieu', a phrase which repeats 'nor ever can those trees be bare', but the new line strengthens the implications of speaking: the falling leaves are a gesture, a word of farewell to the joy of spring. The melodist of Stanza II played sweeter music because unheard, but here, in the third stanza, it is implied that he does not tire of his song for the same reason that the lover does not tire of his love – neither song nor love is consummated. The songs are 'for ever new' because they cannot be completed.

The paradox is carried further in the case of the lover whose love is 'For ever warm and still to be enjoy'd'. We are really dealing with an ambiguity here, for we can take 'still to be enjoy'd' as an adjectival phrase on the same level as 'warm' – that is, 'still virginal and warm'. But the tenor of the whole poem suggests that the warmth of the love depends upon the fact that it has not been enjoyed – that is, 'warm and still to be enjoy'd' may mean also 'warm *because* still to be enjoy'd'.

But though the poet has developed and extended

his metaphors furthest here in this third stanza, the ironic counterpoise is developed furthest too. The love which a line earlier was 'warm' and 'panting' becomes suddenly in the next line, 'All breathing human passion far above'. But if it is *above* all breathing passion, it is, after all, outside the realm of breathing passion, and therefore, not human passion at all.

(If one argues that we are to take 'All breathing human passion' as qualified by 'That leaves a heart high-sorrowful and cloy'd' – that is, if one argues that Keats is saying that the love depicted on the urn is above only that human passion which leaves one cloyed and not above human passion in general, he misses the point. For Keats in the 'Ode' is stressing the ironic fact that all human passion *does* leave one cloyed; hence the superiority of art.)

The purpose in emphasizing the ironic undercurrent in the foregoing lines is not at all to disparage Keats – to point up implications of his poem of which he was himself unaware. Far from it: the poet knows precisely what he is doing. The point is to be made simply in order to make sure that we are completely aware of what he *is* doing. Garrod, sensing this ironic undercurrent, seems to interpret it as an element over which Keats was not able to exercise full control. He says: 'Truth to his main theme [the fixity given by art to forms which in life are impermanent] has taken Keats farther than he meant to go. The pure and ideal art of this "cold Pastoral", this "silent form", *has* a cold silentness which in some degree saddens him. In the last lines of the fourth stanza, especially the last three lines ... every reader is conscious, I should suppose, of an undertone of sadness, of disappointment.' The undertone is there, but Keats had not been taken 'farther than he meant to go'. Keats's attitude, even in the early stanzas, is more complex than Garrod would allow: it is more complex and more ironic, and a recognition of this is important if we are to be able to relate the last stanza to the rest of the 'Ode'. Keats is perfectly aware that the frozen moment of loveliness is more dynamic than is the fluid world of reality *only* because it is frozen. The love depicted on the urn remains warm and young because it is not human flesh at all but cold, ancient marble.

With Stanza IV, we are still within the world depicted by the urn, but the scene presented in this stanza forms a contrast to the earlier scenes. It emphasizes, not individual aspiration and desire, but communal life. It constitutes another chapter in the history that the 'Sylvan historian' has to tell. And again, names and dates have been omitted. We are not told to what god's altar the procession moves, nor the occasion of the sacrifice.

Moreover, the little town from which the celebrants come is unknown; and the poet rather goes out of his way to leave us the widest possible option in locating it. It may be a mountain town, or a river town, or a tiny seaport. Yet, of course, there is a sense in which the nature of the town – the essential character of the town – is actually suggested by the figured urn. But it is not given explicitly. The poet is willing to leave much to our imaginations; and yet the stanza in its organization of imagery and rhythm does describe the town clearly enough; it is small, it is quiet, its people are knit together as an organic whole, and on a 'pious morn' such as this, its whole population has turned out to take part in the ritual.

The stanza has been justly admired. Its magic of effect defies reduction to any formula. Yet, without pretending to 'account' for the effect in any mechanical fashion, one can point to some of the elements active in securing the effect: there is the suggestiveness of the word 'green' in 'green altar' – something natural, spontaneous, living; there is the suggestion that the little town is caught in a curve of the sea-shore, or nestled in a fold of the mountains – at any rate, is something secluded and something naturally related to its terrain; there is the effect of the phrase 'peaceful citadel', a phrase which involves a clash between the ideas of war and peace and resolves it in the senses of stability and independence without imperialistic ambition – the sense of stable repose.

But to return to the larger pattern of the poem: Keats does something in this fourth stanza which is highly interesting in itself and thoroughly relevant to the sense in which the urn is a historian. One of the most moving passages in the poem is that in which the poet speculates on the strange emptiness of the little town which, of course, has not been pictured on the urn at all.

The little town which has been merely implied by the procession portrayed on the urn is endowed with a poignance beyond anything else in the poem. Its streets 'for evermore/Will silent be,' its desolation forever shrouded in a mystery. No one in the figured procession will ever be able to go back to the town to break the silence there, not even one to tell the stranger there why the town remains desolate.

If one attends closely to what Keats is doing here, he may easily come to feel that the poet is indulging himself in an ingenious fancy, an indulgence, however, which is gratuitous and finally silly; that is, the poet has created in his own imagination the town implied by the procession of worshippers, has given it a special character of desolation and loneliness, and then has gone on to treat it as if it were a real town to which a stranger might actually come and be puzzled by its emptiness. (I can see no other interpretation of the lines, 'and not a soul to tell/Why thou art desolate can e'er return.') But, actually, of course, no one will ever discover the town except by the very same process by which Keats has discovered it: namely, through the figured urn, and then, of course, he will not need to ask why it is empty. One can well imagine what a typical eighteenth-century critic would have made of this flaw in logic.

It will not be too difficult, however, to show that Keats's extension of the fancy is not irrelevant to the poem as a whole. The 'reality' of the little town has a very close relation to the urn's character as a historian. If the earlier stanzas have been concerned with such paradoxes as the ability of static carving to convey dynamic action, of the soundless pipes to play music sweeter than that of the heard melody, of the figured lover to have a love more warm and panting than that of breathing flesh and blood, so in the same way the town implied by the urn comes to have a richer and more important history than that of actual cities. Indeed, the imagined town is to the figured procession as the unheard melody is to the carved pipes of the unwearied melodist. And the poet, by pretending to take the town as real – so real that he can imagine the effect of its silent streets upon the stranger who chances to come into it – has suggested in the most powerful way possible its essential reality for him – and for us. It is a case of the doctor's taking his own medicine: the poet is prepared to stand by the illusion of his own making.

With Stanza V we move back out of the enchanted world portrayed by the urn to consider the urn itself once more as a whole, as an object. The shift in point of view is marked with the first line of the stanza by the apostrophe, 'O Attic shape ...' It is the urn itself as a formed thing, as an autonomous world, to which the poet addresses these last words. And the rich, almost breathing world which the poet has conjured up for us contracts and hardens into the decorated motifs on the urn itself: 'with brede/Of marble men and maidens overwrought'. The beings who have a life above life – 'all breathing human passion far above' – are marble, after all.

This last is a matter which, of course, the poet has never denied. The recognition that the men and maidens are frozen, fixed, arrested, has, as we have already seen, run through the second, third, and fourth stanzas as an ironic undercurrent. The central paradox of the poem, thus, comes to conclusion in the phrase, 'Cold Pastoral'. The word 'pastoral' suggests warmth, spontaneity, the natural and the informal as well as the idyllic, the simple, and the informally charming. What the urn tells is a 'flowery tale', a 'leaf-fring'd legend', but the 'sylvan historian' works in terms of marble. The urn itself is cold, and the life beyond life which it expresses is life which has been formed, arranged. The urn itself is a 'silent form', and it speaks, not by means of statement, but by 'teasing us out of thought'. It is as enigmatic as eternity is, for, like eternity, its history is beyond time, outside time, and for this very reason bewilders our time-ridden minds: it teases us.

The marble men and maidens of the urn will not age as flesh-and-blood men and women will: 'When old age shall this generation waste'. (The word 'generation', by the way, is very rich. It means on one level 'that which is generated' – that which springs from human loins – Adam's breed; and yet, so intimately is death wedded to men, the word 'generation' itself has become, as here, a measure of time.) The marble men and women lie outside time. The urn which they adorn will remain. The 'Sylvan historian' will recite its history to other generations.

What will it say to them? Presumably, what it says to the poet now: that 'formed experience', imaginative insight, embodies the basic and fundamental perception of man and nature. The urn is beautiful, and yet its beauty is based – what else is the poem concerned with? – on an imaginative perception of essentials. Such a vision is beautiful but it is also true. The sylvan historian presents us with beautiful histories, and it is a good historian.

Moreover, the 'truth' which the sylvan historian gives is the only kind of truth which we are likely to get on this earth, and, furthermore, it is the only kind that we *have* to have. The names, dates, and special circumstances, the wealth of data – these the sylvan historian quietly ignores. But we shall never get all the facts anyway – there is no end to the accumulation of facts. Moreover, mere accumulations of facts – a point our own generation is only beginning to realize – are meaningless. The sylvan historian does better than that: it takes a few details and so orders them that we have not only beauty but insight into essential truth. Its 'history', in short, is a history without footnotes. It has the validity of myth – not myth as a pretty but irrelevant make-belief, an idle fancy, but myth as a valid perception into reality.

So much for the 'meaning' of the last lines of the 'Ode'. It is an interpretation which defers little from past interpretations. It is put forward here with no pretension to novelty. What is important is the fact that it can be derived from the context of the 'Ode' itself.

And now, what of the objection that the final lines break the tone of the poem with a display of misplaced sententiousness? One can summarize the answer already implied thus: throughout the poem the poet has stressed the paradox of the speaking urn. First, the urn itself can tell a story, can give a history. Then, the various figures depicted upon the urn play music or speak or sing. If we have been alive to these items, we shall not, perhaps, be too much surprised to have the urn speak once more, not in the sense in which it tells a story – a metaphor which is rather easy to accept – but, to have it speak on a higher level, to have it make a commentary on its own nature. If the urn has been properly dramatized, if we have followed the development of the metaphors, if we have been alive to the paradoxes which work throughout the poem, perhaps then, we shall be prepared for the enigmatic, final paradox which the 'silent form' utters. But in that case, we shall not feel that the generalization, unqualified and to be taken literally, is meant to march out of its context to compete with the scientific and philosophical generalizations which dominate our world.

'Beauty is truth, truth beauty' has precisely the same status, and the same justification as Shakespeare's 'Ripeness is all'. It is a speech 'in character' and supported by a dramatic context.

To conclude thus may seem to weight the principle

of dramatic propriety with more than it can bear. This would not be fair to the complexity of the problem of truth in art nor fair to Keats's little parable. Granted; and yet the principle of dramatic propriety may take us further than would first appear. Respect for it may at least insure our dealing with the problem of truth at the level on which it is really relevant to literature. If we can see that the assertions made in a poem are to be taken as part of an organic context, if we can resist the temptation to deal with them in isolation, then we may be willing to go on to deal with the world-view, or 'philosophy', or 'truth' of the *poem as a whole* in terms of its dramatic wholeness: that is, we shall not neglect the maturity of attitude, the dramatic tension, the emotional *and* intellectual coherence in favor of some statement of theme abstracted from it by paraphrase. Perhaps, best of all, we might learn to distrust our ability to represent any poem adequately by paraphrase. Such a distrust is healthy. Keats's sylvan historian, who is not above 'teasing' us, exhibits such a distrust, and perhaps the point of what the sylvan historian 'says' is to confirm us in our distrust.

SOURCE: *The Well-Wrought Urn*, New York and London, 1947; originally published in *Sewanee Review*, LII (1944).

William Empson

THE AMBIGUITY OF 'MELANCHOLY' (1930)

Keats often used ambiguities of this type to convey a dissolution of normal experience into intensity of sensation. This need not be concentrated into an ambiguity.

> Let the rich wine within the goblet boil
> Cold as a bubbling well

is an example of what I mean; and the contrast between cold weather and the heat of passion which is never forgotten throughout 'St Agnes' Eve'. It is the 'going hot and cold at once' of fever. The same method is worth observing in detail when in the 'Ode to Melancholy' it pounds together the sensations of joy and sorrow till they combine into sexuality.

> No, no: go to Lethe, neither twist
> Wolf's-bane, tight-rooted, for its poisonous wine:
> Nor suffer thy pale forehead to be kissed
> By nightshade, ruby grape of Proserpine;
> Make not your rosary of yewberries,
> Nor let the beetle nor the death-moth be
> Your mournful Psyche, nor the downy owl
> A partner in your sorrow's mysteries;
> For shade to shade will come too drowsily,
> And drown the wakeful anguish of the soul.[1]

One must enjoy the didactic tone of this great anthology piece; it is a parody by contradiction, of the wise advice of uncles. 'Of course, pain is what we all desire, and I am sure I hope you will be very unhappy. But if you go snatching at it before your time, my boy, you must expect the consequences; you will hardly get hurt at all.'

'Do not abandon yourself to melancholy, delightful as that would be, or you will lose the sensations of incipient melancholia. Do not think always about forgetting, or you will forget its pain. Do not achieve death, or you can no longer live in its shadow. Taste rather at their most sharp the full sensations of death, of melancholy, and of oblivion.' But I have paraphrased only for my own pleasure; there is no need for me to insist on the contrariety of the pathological splendours of this introduction.

Opposite notions combined in this poem include death and the sexual act, a pair of which I must produce further examples; pain and pleasure, perhaps as a milder version of this; the conception of the woman as at once mistress and mother, at once soothing and exciting, whom one must master, to whom one must yield; a desire at once for the eternity of fame and for the irresponsibility of oblivion; an apprehension of ideal beauty as sensual; and an apprehension of eternal beauty as fleeting. The perfection of form, the immediacy of statement, of the Ode, lie in the fact that these are all collected into the single antithesis which unites Melancholy to Joy. Biographers who attempt to show from Keats's life how he came by these notions are excellently employed, but it is no use calling them in to explain why the poem is so universally intelligible and admired; evidently these pairs of opposites, stated in the right way, make a direct appeal to the normal habits of the mind.

But when the melancholy fit shall fall
    Sudden from Heaven like a weeping cloud,
That fosters the droop-headed flowers all,
    And hides the green hill in an April shroud;

Weeping produces the flowers of joy which are themselves sorrowful; the *hill* is *green* as young, fresh and springing, or with age, mould and geology; *April* is both rainy and part of springtime; and the *shroud*, an anticipation of death that has its own energy and beauty, either is itself the fact that the old *hill* is hidden under *green*, or is itself the grey mist, the greyness of falling rain, which is reviving that verdure.

> Then glut thy sorrow on a morning rose,
> Or on the rainbow of the salt sand-wave,
> Or on the wealth of globed peonies; . . .

Either: 'Give rein to sorrow, at the mortality of beauty,' or 'defeat sorrow by sudden excess and turn it to joy, at the intensity of sensation.' *Morning* is parallel to *April*, and pun with mourning; the flowers stand at once for the more available forms of beauty, and for the *mistress* who is unkind.

> Or if thy mistress some rich anger shows
> Imprison her soft hand, and let her rave,
> And feed deep, deep upon her peerless eyes.
>
> She dwells with Beauty – Beauty that must die;
> And Joy, whose hand is ever at his lips
> Bidding adieu; and aching Pleasure nigh,
> Turning to poison while the bee-mouth sips;
> Aye, in the very temple of Delight
> Veiled Melancholy hath her sovran shrine.

She is at first *thy mistress*, so that she represents some degree of *joy*, however fleeting; then, taking the verse as a unit, she becomes *Veiled Melancholy* itself; *veiled* like a widow or holding up a handkerchief for sorrow, or *veiled*, like the hill under its *green*, because at first sight *joy*. *Very* and *sovran*, with an air of making a distinction and overcoming the casual prejudice of the reader, now insist that this new sort of *joy* is in part a fusion of *joy* and *melancholy*; *sovran* means either 'melancholy is here deepest,' or 'this new production is the satisfactory (and attractive) kind of melancholy';

and she is *veiled* because only in the mystery of her ambivalence is true *joy* to be found.

> Though seen of none save him whose strenuous tongue
> Can burst joy's grape against his palate fine;

'Can burst the distinction between the two opposites; can discover the proud and sated melancholy to which only those are entitled who have completed an activity and achieved joy.'

> His soul shall taste the sadness of her might
> And be among her cloudy trophies hung.

If *sadness* here was taken as an attribute of *melancholy* only, as the only unambiguous reading must insist, we should have a tautology which no amount of historical allusion could make sensible; though *melancholy* meant Burton and Hamlet and *sadness* meant seriousness, it would still be like Coleridge's parody:

> So sad and miff; oh I feel *very* sad.

She has become *joy, melancholy,* and the beautiful but occasionally raving *mistress*; the grandeur of the line is unquestioned only because everybody takes this for granted.

Her trophies (death-pale are they all) are *cloudy* because vague and faint with the intensity and puzzling character of this fusion, or because already dead, or because, though preserved in verse, irrevocable. They are *hung* because sailors on escaping shipwreck hung up votive gifts in gratitude (Horace, III i), or because, so far from having escaped, in the swoon of this achievement he has lost life, independence, and even distinction from her.

No doubt most people would admit that this is how Keats gets his effects, but the words are not obviously ambiguous because, in the general wealth of the writing, it is possible to spread out one to each word the meanings which are actually diffused into all of them.

SOURCE: *Seven Types of Ambiguity*, 1930; text from revised 1947 reprint.

NOTE

1. The whole poem is quoted gradually.

Allen Tate

A READING OF KEATS (1948)

I shall briefly anticipate the end that I am heading towards by setting down a few opinions which will both indicate its direction and gauge my understanding of Keats. 'Lamia' is more closely related to the two great odes, the Nightingale and the Grecian Urn, than to 'Hyperion', and the fact that he could successfully revise 'The Eve of St Agnes' at the time he was finishing 'Lamia' is as much proof as criticism needs that it is not too far from the materials and methods of a poem which some critics would put with the other narratives, 'Isabella' and the fragment 'The Eve of St Mark'. Moreover, we must think of 'Lamia' and 'The Eve of St Agnes' along with the great odes, as follows: 'Ode to a Nightingale', 'Ode on a Grecian Urn', 'Ode to Psyche', 'To Autumn', and 'Ode on Melancholy'. This cluster of poems is the center of Keats's great work, and they all deal with the same imaginative dilemma – or, if we wish to be biographical, the same conflict in Keats's experience. (I cannot agree with Bridges that there is anything in the sonnets as good as the best Shakespeare; I am convinced that they would not have won their great reputation apart from the other work; and I shall not discuss them here.)

The imaginative dilemma of Keats is, I assume, implicit in the poems, which are its best statement: the most that criticism ought to attempt is perhaps a kind of circulatory description of its movements, from poem to poem. Bridges's astute remark that 'Keats's art is primarily objective and pictorial, and whatever other qualities it has are as it were *added on to things as perceived,*' contains critical insight of the first order. I have italicized *added on to things as perceived,* and

I would double the italics of the last two words; they point directly to the imaginative limit of Keats's poetry, one horn of the dilemma out of which it does not move, in which it must, if it is to exceed the *ut pictura, poesis* formula, seek some conversion of that limit.

I should thus offer (for what it is worth) the very general analysis: Keats as a pictorial poet was necessarily presenting in a given poem a series of scenes, and even in the narratives the action does not flow from inside the characters, but is governed pictorially from the outside. He is thus a painting poet and would have earned Lessing's censure. But like every great artist he knew (in his own terms, which are none of our business) that his problem was to work within his limitations, and to transcend them. He was a poet of space whose problem was to find a way of conveying what happens in time; for it is time in which dramatic conflict takes place; and it is only by conversion into dramatic actuality that the parts of the verbal painting achieve relation and significance. 'The form of thought in Keats', says Mr Kenneth Burke, 'is mystical, in terms of an eternal present' – and, I should add, in terms of the arrested action of painting.

When Keats adds to 'things as pèrceived', what does he add? That, it seems to me, is the special problem of Keats. In the simplest language it is the problem of adding movement to a static picture, of putting into motion the 'languor which lingers in the main design' (Bridges) of even the later work.

Of the eight stanzas of 'Ode to a Nightingale' six are distinctly pictorial in method; a seventh, stanza three, in which Keats expresses his complaint of common life, develops as a meditation out of the second stanza, the picture of Provence. The only stanza which does not give us or in some way pertain to a definite scene is number seven; for though the method there is pictorial, the effect is allusive: the permanence of the nightingale's song is established in a rapid series of vignettes, ending with the famous 'faëry lands forlorn'. It is the only stanza, as some critic has remarked, which contains a statement contradictory of our sense of common reality.

> Thou wast not born for death, immortal Bird,

he says to the nightingale; and we cannot agree. The assertion is out of form in an obvious sense; for the poem is an accumulation of pictorial situations; and the claim of immortality for the bird is dramatic and lyrical.

I am raising the question whether the metonymy which attributes to the literal nightingale the asserted immortality of the song is convincing enough to carry the whole imaginative insight of the poem. I think it is, given the limits of Keats's art, but I am still nagged by a difficulty that will not down. It seems to me that the ambivalence of the nightingale symbol contains almost the whole substance of the poem: the bird, as bird, shares the mortality of the world; as symbol, it purports to transcend it. And I feel that the pictorial technique has not been quite dramatic enough to give to the transcendence of the symbol life in some visibly presented experience. The far more implausible, even far-fetched, metaphor of the draughtsman's compasses, in Donne, comes out a little better because through a series of dialectical transformations, from the dying man to the Ptolemaic spheres, and then through the malleable gold to the compasses, there is a progression of connected analogies, given us step by step; and we acknowledge the identity of compasses and lovers as imaginatively possible. Keats merely *asserts*: song equals immortality; and I feel there is some disparity between the symbol and what it is expected to convey – not an inherent disparity, for such is not imaginatively conceivable; but a disparity such as we should get in the simple equation A = B, if we found that the assigned values of A and B were respectively 1 and 3.

This feature of Keats's art we shall find in 'Ode on

a Grecian Urn' but not in 'Ode to Psyche'. I confess that I do not know what to do about this anomalous poem, except to admire it. There appears to me to be very little genuine *sensation* in Keats (rather what Arnold and his contemporaries mistook for sensation), but there is more of it in 'Ode to Psyche' than anywhere else in the great odes. Mr T. S. Eliot puts it first among the odes, possibly because most of its detail is genuinely experienced and because it contains no developed attitude towards life. The other odes do; and it is an attitude less mature than that which Mr Eliot finds in the *Letters*. With this part of his view of Keats one must agree. But it is a dangerous view, since it is very remotely possible that some letters from Shakespeare may turn up some day. But Mr Eliot's preference for 'Ode to Psyche' doubtless shares at bottom the common prejudice that romantic art tends not only to be pictorial but 'off center' and lacking in that appearance of logical structure which we ordinarily associate with Donne and Dryden. I do not want to get into this classical-and-romantic affair, for the usual reason, and for a reason of my own, which is that it has a way of backfiring. Mr Eliot has said that Coleridge and Wordsworth on one side are 'as eighteenth century as anybody'. So is Keats. The apostrophe to the nightingale, which I have been at some pains to try to understand, is quite 'eighteenth century'; but it is not nearly so eighteenth century as the entire third stanza, which I shall now try to understand, assuming that what it says has a close connection with that literal part of the nightingale, the physical bird, which Keats seemed not to know what to do with (except to make it, in the last stanza, fly away). Here it is:

Fade far away, dissolve, and quite forget
  What thou among the leaves hast never known,
The weariness, the fever, and the fret
  Here where men sit and hear each other groan;
Where palsy shakes a few, sad, last gray hairs,

Where youth grows pale, and spectre-thin, and dies;
Where but to think is to be full of sorrow
And leaden-eyed despairs,
Where beauty cannot keep her lustrous eyes,
Or new Love pine at them beyond tomorrow.[1]

Looked at from any point of view, this stanza is bad; the best that one ought to say of it perhaps is that there are worse things in Shelley and Wordsworth, and in Keats himself. (Even Colvin's habitual tone of euology is restrained when he comes to it.[2]) It is bad in the same way as the passages in Shelley's 'Adonais' which exhibit the troops of mourners are bad. Keats here is relapsing into weakened eighteenth-century rhetoric; Blake could have put into the personifications imaginative power, and Pope genuine feeling, or at any rate an elegance and vigor which would have carried them.

There is not space enough in an essay to go into this matter as it needs to be gone into. What I wish to indicate, for the consideration of more thorough readers, is that stanza three may be of the utmost significance in any attempt to understand the structure of Keats's poetry. It gives us a 'picture' of common reality, in which the life of man is all mutability and frustration. But here if anywhere in the poem the necessity to dramatize time, or the pressure of actuality, is paramount. *Keats has no language of his own for this realm of experience.* That is the capital point. He either falls into the poetic language of the preceding age, or, if he writes spontaneously, he commits his notorious errors of taste; in either case the language is not adequate to the feeling; or, to put it 'cognitively', he lacks an ordered symbolism through which he may *know* the common and the ideal reality in a single imaginative act. One would like to linger upon the possible reasons for this. I suspect that evidence from another source, which I shall point out later, will be more telling than anything, even this stanza, that we can find in the odes. The consciousness of change and decay, which can, and did in Keats, inform one of the great modes of poetry, is deeply involved with his special attitude towards sexual love. He never presents love directly and dramatically; it is in terms of Renaissance tapestry, as in 'The Eve of St Agnes', or in a fable of Italian violence, as in 'Isabella'; or, most interesting of all, in terms of a little myth, Lamia the snake-woman, a symbol which permits Keats to objectify the mingled attraction and repulsion which his treatment of love requires. I sometimes think that for this reason 'Lamia' is his best long poem: the symbol inherently contains the repulsive element, but keeps it at a distance, so that he does not have to face it in terms of common experience, his own, or as he was aware of it in his age. Is it saying too much to suppose that Keats's acceptance of the pictorial method is to a large extent connected with his unwillingness to deal with passion dramatically? (There is sensuous detail, but no sensation as direct experience, such as we find in Baudelaire.)

I need not labor a point which even the Victorian critics and biographers, almost without exception, remarked: Keats, both before and after his fatal illness (as other poets have been who were not ill at all) was filled with the compulsive image of the identity of death and the act of love (for example, 'You must be mine to die upon the rack if I want you,' he wrote to Fanny Brawne); and it is only an exaggeration of emphasis to say that death and love are interchangeable terms throughout his poetry. The 'ecstasy' that the nightingale pours forth contains the Elizabethan pun on 'die' with the wit omitted, and a new semi-mystical intensity of feeling added. And is it too much to say that Keats's constant tendency was to face the moment of love only in terms of an ecstasy so intense that he should not survive it? When Lamia vanishes Lycius 'dies'. And this affirmation of life through death is the element that Keats 'adds on to things as perceived'. But life-in-death is presented pictorially, in space, as an eternal moment, not as a moment of dramatic action in time, proceeding from previous action and looking towards its consequences.

The dialectical tension underlying 'Ode to a Nightingale' seems to me to be incapable of resolution, first in terms of Keats's mind as we know it from other sources, and, secondly, in terms of the pictorial technique which dominates the poetic method. This method, which seems to reflect a compulsive necessity of Keats's experience, allows him to present the thesis of his dilemma, the ideality of the nightingale symbol, but not the antithesis, the world of common experience, which is the substance of stanza three. The 'resolution' is suspended in the intensity of the images setting forth the love-death identity and reaching a magnificent climax in stanza six ('Now more than ever seems it rich to die,' etc.). But the climax contains a little less than the full situation; it reaches us a little too simplified, as if Keats were telling us that the best way to live is to die, or the best way to die is to live intensely so that we may die intensely. There may be concealed here one of the oldest syntheses of Christian thought, that we die only to live; but, if so, there has been a marked shrinkage in range of that conception since Donne wrote his 'A Nocturnall upon S. Lucies Day'.

Messrs Brooks and Warren, in their excellent if somewhat confident analysis[3] of the Nightingale ode, argue with much conviction that the dramatic frame of the poem, the painful accession to the trance in the opening lines and the return to immediate reality ('Do I wake or sleep?') at the end, provides a sufficient form. I confess that I am not sure. I am not certain of the meaning of what happens inside the frame; but at times I am not certain that it is necessary to understand it. There is no perfection in poetry. All criticism must in the end be comparative (this does not mean critical relativity); it must constantly refer to what poetry has accomplished in order to estimate what it can accomplish, not what it ought to accomplish; we must heed Mr Ransom's warning that perfect unity or integration in a work of art is a critical delusion. 'Ode to a Nightingale' is by any standard one of the great poems of the world. Our philosophical difficulties with it are not the same as Keats's imaginative difficulties, which pertain to the order of experience and not of reason. The poem is an emblem of one limit of our experience: the impossibility of synthesizing, in the order of experience, the antinomy of the ideal and the real, and, although that antinomy strikes the human mind with a different force in different ages (Donne's dualism is not Keats's), it is sufficiently common to all men in all times to be understood.

If we glance at 'Ode on a Grecian Urn', we shall see Keats trying to unify his pictorial effects by means of direct philosophical statement. 'Do I wake or sleep?' at the end of the Nightingale ode asks the question: Which is reality, the symbolic nightingale or the common world? The famous Truth-Beauty synthesis at the end of the 'Grecian Urn' contains the same question, but this time it is answered. As Mr Kenneth Burke sees it, Truth is the practical scientific world and Beauty is the ideal world above change. The 'frozen' figures on the urn, being both dead and alive, constitute a scene which is at once perceptible and fixed. 'This transcendent scene,' says Mr Burke, 'is the level at which the earthly laws of contradiction no longer prevail.'[4] The one and the many, the eternal and the passing, the sculpturesque and the dramatic, become synthesized in a higher truth. Much of the little that I know about this poem I have learned from Mr Burke and Mr Cleanth Brooks, who have studied it more closely than any other critics; and what I am about to say will sound ungrateful. I suspect that the dialectical solution is Mr Burke's rather than Keats's, and that Mr Brooks's 'irony' and 'dramatic propriety' are likewise largely his own.[5] Mr Brooks rests his case for the Truth-Beauty paradox on an argument for its 'dramatic propriety'; but this is just what I am not convinced of. I find myself agreeing with Mr Middleton

Murry (whom Mr Brooks quotes), who admits that the statement is out of place 'in the context of the poem itself.' I would point to a particular feature, in the last six lines of stanza four, which I feel that neither Mr Burke nor Mr Brooks has taken into a certain important kind of consideration. Here Keats tells us that in the background of this world of eternal youth there is another, from which it came, and that this second world has thus been emptied and is indeed a dead world:

> What little town by river or sea-shore
>   Or mountain-built with peaceful citadel,
>   Is emptied of this folk, this pious morn?
> And, little town, thy streets for evermore
>   Will silent be; and not a soul to tell
>   Why thou art desolate, can e'er return.

Mr Burke quite rightly sees in this passage the key to the symbolism of the entire poem. It is properly the 'constatation' of the tensions of the imagery. What is the meaning of this perpetual youth on the urn? One of its meanings is that it is perpetually anti-youth and anti-life; it is in fact dead, and 'can never return'. Are we not faced again with the same paradox we had in the Nightingale ode, that the intensest life is achieved in death? Mr Burke brings out with great skill the erotic equivalents of the life-death symbols; and for his analysis of the developing imagery throughout we owe him a great debt. Yet I feel that Mr Burke's own dialectical skill leads him to consider the poem, when he is through with it, a philosophical discourse; but it is, if it is anything (and it is a great deal), what is ordinarily known as a work of art. Mr Burke's elucidation of the Truth-Beauty proposition in the last stanza is the most convincing dialectically that I have ever seen; but Keats did not write Mr Burke's elucidation; and I feel that the entire last stanza, except the phrase 'Cold Pastoral' (which probably ought to be somewhere else in the poem) is an illicit commentary added by the poet to a 'meaning' which was symbolically complete at the end of the preceding stanza, number four. Or perhaps it may be said that Keats did to some extent write Mr Burke's elucidation; that is why I feel that the final stanza (though magnificently written) is redundant and out of form.

To the degree that I am guilty with Mr Burke of a prepossession which may blind me to the whole value of this poem (as his seems to limit his perception of possible defects) I am not qualified to criticize it. Here, toward the end of this essay, I glance back at the confession, which I made earlier, of the distance and detachment of my warmest admiration for Keats. It is now time that I tried to state the reasons for this a little more summarily, in a brief comparison of the two fine odes that we have been considering.

Both odes are constructed pictorially in spatial blocks, for the eye to take in serially. Though to my mind this method is better suited to the subject of the Grecian Urn, which is itself a plastic object, than to the Nightingale ode, I take the latter, in spite of the blemishes of detail (only some of which we have looked at), to be the finer poem. If there is not so much in it as in the Grecian Urn for the elucidation of verbal complexity, there is nowhere the radical violation of its set limits that one finds in the last stanza of the Grecian Urn:

> Thou shalt remain, in midst of other woes
> Than ours, a friend to man, to whom thou say'st,
> Beauty is truth, truth beauty, – that is all
> Ye know on earth, and all ye need to know.

It is here that the poem gets out of form, that the break in 'point of view' occurs; and if it is a return to Samuel Johnson's dislike of 'Lycidas' (I don't think it is) to ask how an urn can say anything, I shall have to suffer the consequences of that view. It is Keats himself, of course, who says it; but 'Keats' is here not implicit in the structure of the poem, as he is in 'Ode to a Nightingale'; what he says is what the mathematicians call an extrapolation, an intrusion of matter from another field of discourse, so that even if it be 'true' philosophically it is not a visible function of what the poem says. With the 'dead' mountain citadel in mind, could we not phrase the message of the urn equally well as follows: Truth is *not* beauty, since even art itself cannot do more with death than preserve it, and the beauty frozen on the urn is also dead, since it cannot move. This 'pessimism' may be found as easily in the poem as Keats's comforting paradox. So I should return to the Nightingale ode for its superior *dramatic* credibility, even though the death-life antinomy is not more satisfactorily resolved than in the Grecian Urn. The fall of the 'I' of 'Ode to a Nightingale' into the trance-like meditation in the first stanza and the shocked coming to at the end *ground* the poem in imaginable action, so that the dialectics of the nightingale symbol do not press for resolution. So I confess a reserved agreement with Brooks and Warren.

The outlines of the conflicting claims of the ideal and the actual, in Keats's mind, I have touched upon; but now, with the two great odes in mind, I wish to give those hints a somewhat greater range and try, if possible, to point toward the *kind* of experience with which Keats was dealing when he came up short against the limit of his sensibility, the identity of love and death, or the compulsive image of erotic intensity realizing itself in 'dying'.

One of Keats's annotations to Burton's *Anatomy*, in the copy given him by Brown in 1819, in the great period, is as follows:

> Here is the old plague spot; the pestilence, the raw scrofula. I mean there is nothing disgraces me in my own eyes so much as being one of a race of eyes nose and mouth beings in a planet call'd the earth who all from Plato to Wesley have always mingled goatish winnyish lustful love with the abstract adoration of

> the deity. I don't understand Greek – is the love of God and the Love of women express'd by the same word in Greek? I hope my little mind is wrong – if not I could.... Has Plato separated these lovers? Ha! I see how they endeavour to divide – but there appears to be a horrid relationship.[6]

Keats had just read in Burton the chapter 'Love-Melancholy' in which the two Aphrodites, Urania and Pandemos, appear: there is no evidence that he ever knew more about them than this quotation indicates. Professor Thorpe valiantly tries to show us that Keats must have known from his literary environment something of Plato's doctrine of love, but there is no reason to believe that he ever felt the imaginative shock of reading *The Symposium,* and of experiencing first hand an intuition of a level of experience that the Western world, through Platonism and Christianity, had been trying for more than two millennia to reach. He apparently never knew that the two Aphrodites were merely the subjects of Pausanias's speech, one of the preliminaries to Socrates's great dialectical synthesis. The curious thing about Keats's education is that it was almost entirely literary; he had presumably read very little philosophy and religion. He used the Greek myths, not for the complete (if pagan) religious experience in them, but to find a static and sculpturesque emblem of timeless experience – his own and the experience of his age; hence the pictorial method, and hence the necessity for that method.

In my reading of Keats I see his mind constantly reaching toward and recoiling from the experience, greatly extended, which is represented by the ambivalent Aphrodite. The conclusion of the sonnet 'Bright Star! ...':

> Still, still to hear her tender-taken breath,
> And so live ever – or else swoon to death ...

is not Keats's best poetry, but it states very simply the

conflict of emotion the symbolic limit of which I have tried to see in terms of the double goddess. The immanence of the Uranian in the Pandemic goddess was not beyond the range of Keats's intellect, but it was at any rate, at the time of his death, imaginatively beyond his reach. His goddess, in so far as she is more than a decorative symbol in Keats, was all Uranian; and to say in another way what I have already said, his faulty taste (which is probably at its worst in one of the lines in 'Bright Star! ...') lies in his inability to come to terms with her Pandemic sister. His pictorial and sculpturesque effects, which arrest time into space, tend to remove from experience the dramatic agitation of Aphrodite Pandemos, whose favors are granted and whose woes are counted in the actuality of time. (There is, of course, a great deal more in Keats than this obsessive symbol through which I see him; and there is also less of the symbol, explicitly presented, than my discussion would indicate; there are only eleven references to 'Venus' in all Keats's poetry – he never calls her Aphrodite – and in no instance is very much done with her symbolically. She has only a fresh Botticellian surface; and one may observe that she is not mentioned in 'Ode to Psyche'.)

This 'horrid relationship' between the heavenly and earthly Aphrodites had been in effect the great theme of St Augustine, and before him of Lucretius; and it was to inform dramatically *The Divine Comedy*. It was perhaps the great achievement of the seventeenth-century English poets to have explored the relations of physical and spiritual love; of this Keats seems oblivious; yet we must admit that an awareness of the imaginative and spiritual achievements of the past would not have ensured them to him, as our own excessive awareness fails to ensure them to us. In Keats's mind there was, as I have said (why it should have had, even in so young a man, an exclusive dominance I do not know) – there was, to put it in the simplest language, a strong compulsion towards the realization of physical love, but he could not reconcile it with his idealization of the beloved. So we get what has been supposed to be a characteristically romantic attitude – that to *die* at the greatest intensity of love is to achieve that intensity without diminution. If this is the romantic attitude – and there is no reason to believe that Wordsworth's domestic pieties and evasions, or Shelley's rhetorical Godwinism and watered-down Platonism, ever achieved *as experience* a higher realization of the central human problem than Keats did – if this is romanticism, then romanticism (or romantic poetry) represents a decline in insight and in imaginative and moral power. In the interval between

> So must pure lovers soules descend
>   T'affections, and to faculties,
> Which sense may reach and apprehend,
>   Else a great Prince in prison lies ...

and this:

> But love has pitched his mansion in
> The place of excrement;
> For nothing can be sole or whole
> That has not been rent ...

– between Donne and Yeats there was evidently a shrinkage in the range and depth of Western man's experience, as that experience was expressed in works of the imagination, and not merely in the Goethean or Wordsworthian goodwill towards comprehensiveness or the inclusion of a little of everything. Keats seems to me to have been, in England at any rate, the master of the central experience of his age. His profound honesty, his dislike of system and opinion as substitutes for what the imagination is actually able to control, and his perfect artistic courage, will keep him not only among the masters of English poetry but among the few heroes of literature. To adapt to Keats a remark of Eliot's about Arnold, I should say that he did not know, because he lacked the maturity to know, the boredom; he knew a little of the horror; but he knew much of the glory, of human life.

SOURCE: *On the Limits of Poetry*, 1948, reprinted in *Collected Literary Essays*, Denver, Colorado, 1959.

NOTES

1. Quotations from the poems follow Garrod, *The Poetical Works of John Keats* (Oxford, 1939).
2. Sidney Colvin, *John Keats* (New York, 1917) p. 419.
3. Brooks and Warren, *Understanding Poetry*, pp. 409-15.
4. Kenneth Burke, 'Symbolic Action in a Poem by Keats', *Accent*, vol. IV, no. 1 (autumn 1943) 42.
5. *The Well-Wrought Urn* (New York, 1947) pp. 139-52.
6. I am indebted to a note by Colvin (op. cit., p. 549) for the hint which led me to this bitter confession. It appears in Forman, *The Complete Works of John Keats*, III, 268.
7. Modern readers will find the passage in the edition of Dell and Jordan-Smith (New York, 1927) p. 620.

John Holloway

THE ODES OF KEATS (1952)

In H. W. Garrod's book on Keats there is one sentence about Keats's Odes that is a good deal more pointed and significant than its author presumably intended. Our attention is drawn in it to 'the close connections of thought which exist between all of the ... Odes with the exception of that 'To Autumn ... a sequence ... not of time but of mood'.[1] The reader's first reaction, perhaps, will be suspicion of that unremarked shift from 'thought' to 'mood'; his second, that if this is an evasion, it comes near to solving the difficulty it evades. What unites these poems is essentially a singleness in experience; and in a sense it is too elusive for the first word, but too considered, too developed, too much articulated for the second. Yet if the Odes really are a unified sequence, the best way to understand them fully is to treat them as such, and make them interpret each other. So far, this has hardly been done – in part because critics have been too ready to think (as Garrod did) that 'To Autumn' stands quite by itself, and in part because they have thought 'On Indolence' too bad to deserve much attention. These restrictions of interest are precipitate; and a more systematic inquiry not only offers a more sensitive, balanced, comprehensive interpretation of each poem by itself, but seems to do something in addition. It seems also to show that these poems collectively make up a psychological document – an unexpected one – of unique interest. To a great extent, they are actually about that part of Keats's mental life of most significance to both him and us. They prove to be a complex and detailed poetic revelation of what Keats knew himself as the creative mood. The present study, then, has a double purpose: to add to our insight into the Odes as poems, and to indicate just how much they reveal of Keats the writer.

Let us begin with the Ode 'On Indolence', though only because its language is baldest and simplest. To trace a genuinely chronological development through the Odes, it would be necessary to show, if we took this as a starting-point, that it was written first; and this may very well not be true, though the evidence is less conclusive than Miss Lowell, for example, seemed to think.[2] But my purpose is rather to identify, as definitely as can be done, a mood which seems to underlie all the Odes, and appears in them sometimes in a more, sometimes (and 'On Indolence' is an example) in a less developed form. Besides this, however, Keats's *Letters* make it clear that on 19 March 1819 (at the beginning of the period in which all these poems were written) he was not only in the exact mood of 'On Indolence', but could almost paraphrase the poem in prose:

> ... This morning I am in a sort of temper indolent and supremely careless: I long after a stanza or two of Thompson's Castle of Indolence. My passions are all asleep from my having slumbered till nearly eleven and weakened the animal fibre all over to a delightful sensation about three degrees this side of faintness – if I had teeth of pearl and the breath of lillies I should call it langour – but as I am I must call it Laziness. In this state of effeminacy the fibres of the brain are relaxed in common with the rest of the body, and to such a happy degree that pleasure has no show of enticement and pain no unbearable frown. Neither Poetry, nor Ambition, nor Love have any alertness of countenance as they pass me by: they seem rather like three figures on a greek vase – a Man and two women whom no one but myself could distinguish in their disguisement. This is the only happiness; and it is a rare instance of advantage in the body overpowering the Mind.[3]

So much for prose. The poem could scarcely do

more to convey the same ideas. Keats affirms that neither Love, Ambition nor Poetry has charm enough to tempt him from a mood of exquisite somnolence, when

> ... ripe was the drowsy hour;
> The blissful cloud of summer-indolence
> Benumb'd my eyes.

Both pain and pleasure seem to vanish, and they leave only a simple sensuous awareness, calm and yet somehow keen:

> The open casement pressed a new-leav'd vine
> Let in the budding warmth and throstle's lay.

This is all plain enough. Keats's mood is not subtle or complex, and it does not develop in the course of the poem. What is significant is that several turns of phrase or thought in this Ode reappear in the others; and there are elements of something that is more complex and that does develop. Of these, the drowsy indolence is of course one; so is the idea that Ambition is worthless because coming

> From a man's little heart's short fever-fit;...

The indolent mood which is the source of the poem, and somehow mingles sleeping and waking, is not lethargy but in some sense a visionary state; not devoid of pleasure and pain, but transmuting them:

> Pain had no sting, and pleasure's wreath no flower.

Pain and pleasure have not ceased entirely, but ceased only to be disturbances, superficial additions to life. Poetry, which seems for the moment only 'my demon Poesy', the strongest of temptations,

has not a joy
At least for me – so sweet as drowsy noons
And evenings steeped in honey'd indolence.

And this indolence is a positive thing, bringing a calm pervasive happiness that – its crucial feature perhaps – seems near to a suspension of sense for some other more elusive but more illuminating kind of experience:

O, why did ye not melt, and leave my sense
Unhaunted quite of all but – nothingness?

'On Indolence' seems at first to reject poetry, but it is really a poem about the mood from which Keats's poetry at that time sprang. That this was consciously in Keats's mind is to some extent confirmed by one of the sonnets 'On Fame', probably written at about this time:

Fame like a wayward Girl will still be coy
To those who woo her with too slavish knees ...

Make your best bow to her and bid adieu
Then if she likes it she will follow you.[4]

The 'Ode to Psyche' clarifies the situation. Keats's mood here is much like the mood of 'On Indolence':

Surely I dream't today, or did I see
The winged Psyche with awaken'd eyes?
I wandered in a forest thoughtlessly
And, on the sudden, fainting with surprise
Saw two fair creatures ...

– here is the same inertia and oblivion and suspension between sleeping and waking. When he finds Cupid and the goddess 'in soft-handed slumber' together

'Mid hush'd cool-rooted flowers fragrant-eyed
Blue, silver-white, and budded Tyrian
They lay calm-breathing on the bedded grass

this is almost exactly like his own condition in 'On Indolence';[5] and the interaction between Keats's own emotions, and the emotions of his subject, will prove later to be an important aspect of the 'Ode to a Nightingale'. Keats has a good phrase in 'To Psyche' for the central quality of his feeling: 'this wide quietness'. But as the poem proceeds, drowsy numbness is raised, as it were, to a higher power of itself:

> I see, and sing, by my own eyes inspired.

Keats is inspired to sing through seeing the goddess (especially, one is sorry to say, through seeing her 'lucent fans'). He desires to serve the deity of a mood whose expression is more complex, more impassioned, and indeed more intellectual, than anything in 'On Indolence'. His mood tends towards activity, it is a balanced tension of excitement, and here unmistakably it has something of an intellectual insight, a fuller understanding:

> ... I will be thy priest, and build a fane
> In some untrodden region of my mind
> Where branched thoughts, new grown with pleasant pain
> ... shall murmur.
>
> A rosy sanctuary will I dress
> With the wreath'd trellis of a working brain
>
> And there shall be for thee all soft delight
> That shadowy thought can win.

The stress falls largely on the melancholic aspects of Psyche the Love-goddess (she is called 'mournful Psyche' in 'On Melancholy'); Keats laments that she has no

> ... virgin-choir to make delicious moan
> Upon the midnight hours; ...

But the 'wide quietness' of this poem has a certain poignancy, and as the mood develops, Keats's tone becomes more complex and at the same time more incisive.

For all that, however, the genesis of the poem still lies in 'softhanded slumber'; and that this originates the whole sequence of experience is suggested once more at the beginning of the 'Ode On Melancholy'. The oblivion of Lethe is too uncompromising, wolfsbane too powerful a narcotic, the death moth too grim and macabre to incarnate 'mournful Psyche'. These are extreme measures that the mood cannot survive:

> ... shade to shade will call too drowsily
> And drown the wakeful anguish of the soul ...

The 'melancholy fit' falls suddenly, like an April shower 'that fosters the droop-headed flowers all'; and like the shower, Melancholy has its own reviving virtue. In this mood we are to 'glut' sorrow in the contemplation of beautiful things, 'feed; deep, deep' on them; and that our experience will also be an insight.

The last stanza suggests how. 'She dwells with Beauty –' whether 'she' is the imagined mistress, or the goddess of Melancholy, or both or either, leaves the sense unaffected. The experience of Beauty is a revelation; of Beauty's meaning, and also of its transience. Melancholy is developed here to a keener, tenser equipoise of sorrow and uncertainty, and also of exaltation and elusive understanding:

> ... Beauty that must die;
> And Joy, whose hand is ever at his lips
> Bidding adieu; and aching Pleasure nigh
> Turning to poison while the bee-mouth sips:
> Ay, in the very temple of Delight
> Veil'd Melancholy has her sovran shrine
> Though seen of none save him whose strenuous tongue

Can burst Joy's grape against his palate fine:
His soul shall taste the sadness of her might,
And be among her cloudy trophies hung.

This is very different from the drowsy numbness of 'Indolence', and its 'strenuous tongue' is like the 'working brain' of 'To Psyche'. But the last two lines have a special interest: 'cloudy trophies' may hint at the elusiveness of the insight that dwells with Beauty, but the cadence of this couplet causes it, and therefore the whole stanza, to exemplify what it describes. The reader watches Joy bidding adieu, because he is taken through the experience of which the poem gives an account.

Of these three Odes, 'On Indolence' in the main portrays a mood which is the embryo of the 'melancholy fit', 'To Psyche' celebrates the deity of one of its forms (love-melancholy), and 'On Melancholy' displays its growth and intensity and climax. The other two – perhaps the other three – Odes centre upon particular things which have evoked or represented the experience for Keats himself. To a very considerable degree they run parallel – though this has been overlooked by several critics, or expressly denied; and they have many features in common with the three Odes discussed so far. Thus in the opening lines of 'To a Nightingale' the drowsy numbness is, once more, both an aching pain and a too-sharp happiness; hearing the song induces Keats to forget and also remember what is unhappy in life – it brings oblivion that, at a deeper level, is keener knowledge. Once again the senses are stilled, but to an 'embalmed darkness' that is even so a heightened sensuous awareness divining the surrounding sensuous wealth; and when Keats thinks of 'easeful Death' it is like 'nothingness' in 'On Indolence' – as the completion of this unique oblivion.

No one seems quite to have explained the imaginative movement of the poem at the point where Keats makes the nightingale immortal. Bridges regarded this passage as fanciful, and Miss Lowell as Platonic.[6]

Garrod, avoiding these errors, suggests that the nightingale is immortal because Keats thinks of it as a Dryad.[7] But why is it appropriate to think the bird immortal for any reason? Why should we not suppose ourselves confronted here with irresponsible, fanciful ingenuity? The answer is, perhaps, that at the climax of his poem Keats rightly allows a new ease of movement within the set of ideas he is controlling: he uses a freedom of contribution which characterizes poetry at high temperatures, as I believe it does chemistry (in both cases, oddly enough, *constitutes* is perhaps an apter word). The nightingale momentarily assumes the qualities of that ecstasy which it seems to experience, and which it induces in Keats. Within the apparently irresponsible movement of the stanza runs an exact line of what I am almost tempted to call logical development. Keats, entranced as he listens to the nightingale and responds to its apparent ecstasy, has an experience that seems to him to transcend experience; and in this stanza he claims that the nightingale's song is unrestricted by either time or space – which after all are pervasive features of experience. The voice of the nightingale, we might put it, is made immune first to history, and then to geography: it can establish a *rapport* with dead generations or with faery lands; and

> ... the same that oft-times hath
> Charm'd magic casements, opening on the foam
> Of perilous seas, in faery lands forlorn

is not Romantic escapism or idle gesturing. Word by word, this passage, in the free way of poetry, is indicating the definite qualities of what was for Keats something he knew: the magic, the 'wideness', the heightened tension, the sadness, are things that we have by now traced elsewhere.

But like the 'Ode on Melancholy', this poem represents the experience it describes, and represents it without abridgement; it gives not only the genesis and progress and climax, but also the dissolution, of the mood that seems central to all the Odes. Garrod's belief[8] that at this point Keats's poem may have owed something to Wordsworth's *Solitary Reaper* is probably correct; but it leads him to say of

> ... thy plaintive anthem fades

that it is 'the only false note which the Ode discovers'. Here a too full knowledge of the psychology of composition appears to have confused a quite separate question of criticism; reading this poem in the light of the other Odes makes it clear that 'plaintive' is here no false but the exactly right note. If it were false, so would be 'faery lands forlorn'. Forlorn they might be, but they would then intrude. They do not, because as ever the magic dissolves in its own moment of existence:

> Turning to poison while the bee-mouth sips

– and the very last words of the poem, with their uncertainty between waking and sleeping, are not in opposition to what has gone before, but express something that is integral to the situation, and that has appeared in every Ode so far. The poem has reverted from its climax to a calmer mood not altogether remote from the mood of its origin.

Garrod and Miss Lowell have both assumed a contrast between 'To a Nightingale' and 'On a Grecian Urn'.[9] Miss Lowell sees a 'direct antithesis'; Garrod describes 'On a Grecian Urn' as written in 'strong revulsion' from the mood of 'On Melancholy', and of this poem in fairly close sympathy with 'To a Nightingale'. But it is rather doubtful whether the difference is more than a shift of emphasis. Miss Lowell's account, 'realization of the eternal quality of art binds and heals the bitter wounds incident upon mere living', suggests that 'On a Grecian Urn' is a vicarious *exegi monumentum*. Garrod's view is not unlike this: 'the "Grecian Urn" presents ... the world of beauty and human passions, only fixed by art.' He speaks of its 'rather formal philosophy'. 'The theme of . . . (the first four stanzas) . . . is the arrest of beauty, the fixity given by art to forms which in life are fluid and impermanent, and the appeal of art from the senses to the spirit. The theme of the final stanza is the relation of beauty to truth, to thought.' These views distort the poem. It has no rather formal philosophy'. It as much expresses a mood as 'To a Nightingale'; but the mood is modulated to the different object which inspires it. Between the nightingale and the urn is the difference of embalmed darkness and perpetual spring or summer; but 'Veil'd Melancholy' is never wholly absent from 'On a Grecian Urn', though too much veiled, it seems, for some critics. There is a hint of her even in the 'maidens loth' and 'struggle to escape' and the 'wild ecstasy' of the first stanza; in the second comes the eternal frustration of the dancers; their eternal freedom, in the third, perhaps makes the poet happy in sympathy, but it is happiness that trembles upon passionate regret; stanza four contrasts the eternal grace of the figures and the eternal silence and desolation of their 'little town'; and the last stanza contrasts the kindly wisdom of the urn with the waste and frustration of ordinary life. Throughout the poem, then, this antithesis is maintained. The lovers and the musicians are protected from humanity's disillusionments only through being denied its rewards. Their triumph, so far as they have one, is in the realised perfection of a single poignant and yet gracious moment. This moment embraces the same fusion of quiet ('thou still unravished bride of quietness') and wild ecstasy, the same exquisite but precarious balance of grief and happiness, the same eternalization of a passing moment, that Keats himself knew in 'To a Nightingale'. In 'On a Grecian Urn' he is describing, as he sees it in others, what in the former poem he experienced and expressed for himself. The experience is not, of course, identical; but the type is unchanged. Keats is now the recorder, in the other poem he was the protagonist. It would simplify to say that this was a full account. The nightingale was also in ecstasy, and to some extent the loneliness of the little town and of the dancer's raptures are contagious. But the urn-figures are a fuller manifestation of this rapture than the nightingale, and there is a different balance in the two poems between the poet's own mood and the object evoking it.

Garrod was critical of the words 'cold pastoral', as a departure from all that had gone before,[10] but they are, on the contrary, an exact continuation. The sculpted pipes play 'ditties of no tone' to the mind's ear only; and this coldness is not the source only in plain fact of the dancer's ecstatic permanence, for it evokes also something that is central to that ecstasy. Cleanth Brooks's account, 'the scene is one of violent love-making',[11] is to say the least of it premature; it ignores the subtlety and elaboration of Keats's scene, and how carefully (even before we reach the altar and the priest) he marshalls the imaginative elements which make the whole poem, and nothing less than that, explain those so-much-discussed lines. He does this once again in saying that the urn can 'tease us out of thought *As doth eternity*': it leads, not to no thought, but to a unique kind of thought. And when Cleanth Brooks writes that the urn says 'imaginative insight embodies the basic and fundamental perception ... the urn is beautiful, and yet its beauty is based ... on an imaginative perception of essentials'[12] no doubt he is right. This does summarize, in abstract form, what Keats told his reader in the concrete form of poetry. But to gloss this with 'mere accumulations of facts ... are meaningless' is to get away from the poem again. Keats glossed it by writing the whole Ode to convey what he thought an imaginative perception of essentials was like. A kind of peace, a kind of excitement, a kind of regret, a kind of ecstasy, an insight that seemed central and yet was strangely like oblivion – the list may briefly remind the successful reader of what he found in the poem, but prose, of course, must say obscurely what poetry says clearly.

There is one poem of Keats which throws light of particular importance on the Odes. This is the sonnet 'Why did I laugh tonight?' which we know, from the *Letters*, must have been written shortly before 19 March, 1819, and therefore near the beginning of this creative period. It is important for three reasons: it hints at some of the antimonies which the present enquiry has emphasized, it declares that ecstasy is inseparable from physical experience, which we saw Keats recognizing as the embryo of 'On Indolence', and it has verbal parallels with no less than three of the Odes. 'Nothing ever becomes real until it is experienced' Keats writes, immediately before copying out this poem for George and Georgina Keats.[13] And then:

Why did I laugh tonight? No voice can tell:
  No God no Demon of severe response,
Deigns to reply from Heaven or from Hell. –
  Then to my human heart I turn at once –
Heart! thou and I are here sad and alone;
  I say, why did I laugh? O mortal pain!
O Darkness! Darkness! ever must I moan,
  To question Heaven and Hell and Heart in vain!
Why did I laugh? I know this Being's lease
  My fancy to its utmost blisses spreads:
Yet could I on this very midnight cease
  And the world's gaudy ensigns see in shreds;
Verse, Fame and Beauty are intense indeed
But Death intenser – Death is Life's high meed.

Lines 9-10 repeat, perhaps rather obscurely, the 'advantage in the body overpowering the mind' which Keats referred to in describing his indolent mood of 19th March; and it has often been noted how line 11 resembles 'to cease upon the midnight with no pain' of 'To a Nightingale'. But critics have not usually noticed that the gaudy ensigns in shreds have clearly something in common with the 'cloudy trophies' of 'On Melancholy' (though the two images are put almost to contrary use in the two poems); and, more important, that the 'Verse, fame and Beauty' of line 13 are virtually the same as the 'Poetry, Ambition and Love' of 'On Indolence'. Both by its wording and by its substance, therefore, this sonnet does something further to suggest that the Odes explore various phases of a single experience.

Any similar suggestion about 'To Autumn' must be very tentative. Keats composed the other poems within a brief period in the spring and early summer of 1819, and this not until several months later. It may well have arisen from a quite independent poetic impulse. But it is not altogether fanciful, perhaps, to see it as a quiet and gentle close to the whole sequence of poems, standing to them all somewhat as the last three lines of 'On a Grecian Urn' stand to that single poem. Nor would it be difficult to point out details that are reminiscent of the Odes – Autumn drowsing with the fumes of poppies (drowsing, too, among the 'twined flowers', like Keats himself in 'On Indolence' or the goddess in 'To Psyche'), or Keats's rejection of the songs of spring, or perhaps even the mourning choirs of gnats. But however this may be, stressing the affinity serves one indisputably useful purpose: it shows that 'To Autumn' is totally different from the descriptive poem of a catalogue kind. Keats has given in it a quite selective picture of autumn, and one that conveys a quite distinctive mood. How far the earlier poems have made us familiar with the analogues of this mood is perhaps an open question.

All in all, Miss Lowell was rash to say, of 'On Indolence', 'this, of course, was pure fatigue'.[14] It seems much more like an expression of the very frame of mind from which at this time, to varying degrees on various occasions, Keats found the raptures of poetic inspiration generate themselves – and do so, moreover, exactly because he was not seeking them. The other Odes document various aspects of this process of generation. Sir Maurice Bowra, writing 'the three stanzas in which Keats tells of the timeless moments depicted on the Urn arise from his own knowledge of what creation is'[15] seems to suggest this also. And there are, of course, well-known passages in Keats's *Letters* which indicate that he regarded what might be called the embryonic condition of the mood conveyed by these poems as also the embryo of poetic inspiration. 'As to the poetical Character itself (I mean that sort of which, if I am anything, I am a Member ...) it has no self – it is everything and nothing – it has no character – it enjoys light and shade';[16] 'if Poetry comes not as naturally as the Leaves on a tree it had better not come at all'.[17] In a word, the Odes are not only products of what Keats himself called 'Negative Capability', but taken together are a uniquely full account of what it is like and how it develops.

SOURCE: *Cambridge Journal*, v (April 1952); reprinted in *The Charted Mirror*, 1960.

NOTES

1. H. W. Garrod, *Keats* (1926) p. 97.
2. A. Lowell, *John Keats*, II 258.
3. *Letters*, ed. M. B. Forman, 2nd ed. (1935) p. 315. Miss D. Hewlett (*A Life of John Keats*, 2nd ed. p. 244) writes 'when he (Keats) wrote, or finished, the "Ode on Indolence" in May the man and two women ... became three female figures'. But while the poem is explicit that Love and Poesy are 'maidens' there is nothing to show that Keats is thinking of Ambition as female, and a little perhaps to show that he is not.
4. *Letters*, p. 338 (30 April 1819).
5. ... Ye cannot raise
   My head cool-bedded from the flowery grass.
6. *John Keats. A Critical Essay* (1895), quoted in Lowell, op. cit., II, 252 (Miss Lowell's own discussion of the poem).
7. Op. cit., p. 114.
8. Op. cit., p. 115.
9. Garrod, op. cit., pp. 104, 108; Lowell, op. cit., II 247.

10. Op. cit., p. 106.
11. *The Well-Wrought Urn*, p. 143.
12. *The Well-Wrought Urn*, p. 150.
13. *Letters*, p. 316.
14. Op. cit., II 258.
15. *The Romantic Imagination*, p. 142.
16. *Letters*, p. 227 (27 October 1818).
17. Ibid., p. 108 (27 February 1818).

Leonard Unger

KEATS AND THE MUSIC OF AUTUMN (1956)

With the possible exception of Coleridge, who has loomed large as a critic, the reputation of no romantic poet has in our century maintained so steady a course as that of John Keats. While Wordsworth, Byron, and Shelley were being attacked or neglected, Keats was spared, mentioned with a special deference, and even given admiring critical analysis and scholarly study. In recent years especially has his better work, so often designated 'the great odes', received serious critical attention. F. R. Leavis, Kenneth Burke, Cleanth Brooks, and Allen Tate have all made appraisals and interpretations of one or more of these poems. 'Ode to a Nightingale' and 'Ode on a Grecian Urn' have been of central interest and received the fullest examination, and this is in no way surprising. It is my impression, however, that 'To Autumn' has been peculiarly neglected, that it merits greater attention, both in its own right and for its significance in the interrelatedness of all the odes, than it has received. For example, there is not a single reference to it in James R. Caldwell's excellent book *John Keats' Fancy*. Tate, in an essay primarily concerned with the Nightingale ode, writes of 'To Autumn' that it 'is a very nearly perfect piece of style but it has little to say'. This is true enough in a sense, yet I propose that it is not true in the sense in which Tate must surely be using the word *say* about a poem. Leavis, in an essay on Keats' later work, quotes Middleton Murry on 'To Autumn': 'It is a perfect and unforced utterance of the truth contained in the magic words: "Ripeness is all."' And then Leavis makes this comment: 'Such talk is extravagant, and does not further the appreciation of Keats. No one could have found that order of significance in the Ode merely by inspecting the Ode itself. The ripeness with which Keats is concerned is the physical ripeness of autumn, and his genius manifests itself in the sensuous richness with which he renders this in poetry, without the least touch of artistic over-ripeness.' Leavis, too, is of the opinion that the poem *says* little. But I believe that Murry's comment on the poem shows a valid and demonstrable insight into a part of its meaning.

Leavis' seeming dictum that we should read a poem merely by itself is both surprising and confusing. I am not prepared to say where the legitimate context of a poem begins and ends, but I would argue that a poem need not and sometimes cannot be read in such isolation. It is common enough for a reader to return to the same poem several times over the years, and to find new orders of significance. He might expand, or somehow qualify, the meaning he first found by simply using a dictionary during the second reading. After we have some familiarity with Homer, can we read the *Odyssey* as if we had never heard of the *Iliad*? Perhaps Leavis has arrived at this fallacy because Keats is close to us in time, so that his individual poems, on one order of significance, are wholly available. But surely no amount of footnoting or scholarly introduction can provide the kind of illumination for the individual poem, whether Petrarch's or Yeats', which it receives from the other works of its author, and even from the works of other authors – and finally from the stage of literacy, the general fund of knowledge, which a particular reader brings to a poem. The scholar can, of course, provide some relevant signposts and reminders. Modern critics, Leavis among them, have done a truly good deed in rescuing poetry from the morgue of scholarship *pour* scholarship, but when the poem is isolated for close analysis it may remain something less than restored if too much emphasis is put on the isolation. Although there are no 'authorities' on this question, it is interesting to recall that two critics who have led the way toward the analytical interpretation of poetry also insisted on the reverse of isolation. In that early and long famous essay on tradition, Eliot announced that 'no poet ... has his complete meaning alone', and his arguments are applicable to the individual poem. Ransom, evaluating and interpreting *Lycidas* in two of his earlier essays, looks backward and forward in Milton's work and suggests that the poem is 'nearly anonymous'. That the whole is greater than the sum of its parts is true not only of a poem but of a poet's whole work – or rather, this is true of better poems, and of poets whose achievement is most formidable. Fortunately, Leavis' own practice as a critic is not limited by the principle of reading a poem 'merely by itself'. As I read 'To Autumn' in the light of Keats' other poems, I shall also be working in an illumination kindled by all the writers mentioned above.

It seems generally agreed that 'To Autumn' is a rich and vivid description of nature, expertly achieved within a fairly intricate stanzaic pattern. The words are successfully descriptive (or evocative) in their phonetic qualities and rhythmical arrangement, as well as in their imagistic references. If we are familiar with Keats' other work, however, we can discover that the poem is not only rich in pictorial and sensuous details, but that it has a depth of meaning and a characteristic complexity of structure. 'To Autumn' is allied especially to the odes on Melancholy, on a Grecian Urn, and to a Nightingale. The four poems are various treatments presenting differing aspects of a single theme.

In so far as the theme is 'stated' in any of the poems, it is most clearly stated in the 'Ode on Melancholy'. In fact, if we want a general formulation of the theme, we need only quote the last stanza – especially these lines:

> Ay, in the very temple of Delight
>   Veil'd Melacholy has her sovran shrine,

Though seen of none save him whose strenuous
tongue
Can burst Joy's grape against his palate fine.

Keats was obviously preoccupied with the consideration that beauty and melancholy are closely related: true melancholy is to be found only in the fullness of living, in beauty, joy and delight, for these experiences make most poignant the passage of time, through which such experiences and then life itself must come to an end.

All this is clear enough in the 'Ode on Melancholy'. There is, however, the implication that the relationship between beauty and melancholy works both ways. That is, either joy or sadness is most intensely felt when it is attended by a consciousness of the experience which is opposite and yet so closely related to it. The theme, then, is more complex and subtle than the aspect of it which appears on the surface in 'Ode on Melancholy'. Other implications of the theme may be found throughout the four poems, which illuminate and clarify each other. This is not to say that the poems are merely repetitions of the same theme, which Keats had in mind before he wrote any of them. When we understand the poems we might find it more accurate to say that each is the exploration of a certain theme.

With so much of its context in mind, let us examine closely 'To Autumn'. The poem opens with an apostrophe to the season, and with a description of natural objects at their richest and ripest stage.

Season of mists and mellow fruitfulness,
Close bosom-friend of the maturing sun;
Conspiring with him how to load and bless
With fruit the vines that round the thatch-eaves
run;
To bend with apples the moss'd cottage-trees,
And fill all fruit with ripeness to the core;
To swell the gourd, and plump the hazel shells

With a sweet kernel; to set budding more.
  And still more, later flowers for the bees,
  Until they think warm days will never cease,
    For Summer has o'er-brimmed their clammy
    cells.

The details about the fruit, the flowers and the bees constitute a lush and colorful picture of autumn and the effects of the 'maturing sun'. In the final lines of the first stanza, however, slight implications about the passage of time begin to operate. The flowers are called 'later', the bees are assumed to think that 'warm days will never cease', and there is a reference to the summer which has already past.

In the second stanza, an imaginative element enters the description, and we get a personification of the season in several appropriate postures and settings.

Who hath not seen thee oft amid thy store?
  Sometimes whoever seeks abroad may find
Thee sitting careless on a granary floor,
  Thy hair soft-lifted by the winnowing wind;
Or on a half-reap'd furrow sound asleep,
  Drows'd with the fume of poppies, while thy hook
    Spares the next swath and all its twinèd flowers;
And sometimes like a gleaner thou dost keep
  Steady thy laden head across a brook;
  Or by a cyder-press, with patient look,
    Thou watchest the last oozings hours by hours.

As this stanza proceeds, the implications of the descriptive details become increasingly strong. For example, autumn is now seen, not as setting the flowers to budding, but as already bringing some of them to an end, although it 'Spares the next swath'. Autumn has become a 'gleaner'. The whole stanza presents the paradoxical qualities of autumn, its aspects both of lingering and passing. This is specially true of the final image. Autumn is the season of dying as well as of fulfilling. Hence it is with '*patient* look' that she (or he?) watches the last oozings hours by hours'. Oozing, or a steady dripping, is, of course, not unfamiliar as a symbol of the passage of time.

It is in the last stanza that the theme emerges most conspicuously.

> Where are the songs of Spring? Ay, where are they?
> Think not of them, thou hast thy music too, –
> While barred clouds bloom the soft-dying day,
> And touch the stubble-plains with rosy hue;
> Then in a wailful choir the small gnats mourn
> Among the river sallows, borne aloft
> Or sinking as the light wind lives or dies;
> And full-grown lambs loud bleat from hilly bourn;
> Hedge-crickets sing; and now with treble soft
> The red-breast whistles from a garden-croft;
> And gathering swallows twitter in the skies.

The opening question implies that the season of youth and rebirth, with its beauties of sight and sound, has passed, and that the season of autumn is passing. But autumn, too, *while* it lasts – 'While barred clouds bloom the soft-dying day' – has its beauties, its music, as Keats' poem demonstrates. The imagery of the last stanza contrasts significantly with that of the first, and the final development of the poem adds meaning to its earlier portions. The slight implications are confirmed. We may recall that 'maturing' means aging and ending as well as ripening. The earlier imagery is, of course, that of ripeness. But the final imagery is more truly autumnal. The first words used to describe the music of autumn are 'wailful' and 'mourn'. The opening stanza suggests the height of day, when the sun is strong and the bees are gathering honey from the open flowers. But in the last stanza, after the passing of 'hours and hours', we have 'the soft-dying day', the imagery of sunset and deepening twilight, when the clouds impart their glow to the day and the plains. The transitive, somewhat rare use of the verb *bloom,* with its springlike associations, is perhaps surprising, and certainly appropriate and effective in suggesting the tensions of the theme, in picturing a beauty that is lingering, but *only* lingering. The conjunction of 'rosy hue' and 'stubble-plains' has the same significant incongruity, although the image is wholly convincing and actual in its reference. While the poem is more descriptive and suggestive than dramatic, its latent theme of transitoriness and mortality is symbolically dramatized by the passing course of the day. All these characteristics of the poem are to be found in its final image: 'And gathering swallows twitter in the skies'. Here we have the music of autumn. And our attention is directed toward the darkening skies. Birds habitually gather in flocks toward nightfall, particularly when they are preparing to fly south at the approach of winter. But they are still gathering. The day, the season, are 'soft-dying' and are both the reality and the symbol of life as most intensely and poignantly beautiful when viewed from this melancholy perspective.

This reading of 'To Autumn' is obviously slanted in the direction of a theme which is also found in the other odes. The theme is, of course, only a part of the poem, a kind of dimension, or extension, which is almost concealed by other features of the poem, particularly by the wealth of concrete descriptive detail. Whereas in 'Ode on Melancholy' the theme, in one of its aspects, is the immediate subject, in 'To Autumn' the season is the subject and the details which describe and thus present the subject are also the medium by which the theme is explored. It may be of interest, at this point, to distinguish between exploration and illustration. For example, Herrick's 'To Daffodils' has a theme which is at least superficially similar to Keats'. But in Herrick's poem the theme is openly stated, and it is, in fact, the subject, which is illustrated by logical analogy with the daffodils. In 'To Autumn', however, the relationship between subject and theme is not one of analogy. The theme inheres in the subject, and is at no point stated in other terms. That is why we could say, in our reading of the poem, that the subject 'is both the reality and the symbol', and to say now that the development of the subject is, in a respect, the exploration of a theme.

The poem has an obvious structure in so far as it is a coherent description. Its structure, however, is not simple in the sense of being merely continuous. For example, the course of the day parallels the development of the poem. And an awareness of the theme gives even greater significance to the structure, for the theme emerges with increasing clarity and fullness throughout the poem until the very last line. Because the theme is always in the process of emerging without ever shaking off the medium in which it is developed, the several parts of the poem have a relationship to each other beyond their progression in a single direction. The gathering swallows return some borrowed meaning to the soft-dying day with substantial interest, and the whole last stanza negotiates with the first in a similar relationship. (If we had a special word for this kind of structure in poetry, we should be less inclined to discuss it figuratively. The words *organic* and *dynamic* have been used, as well as the word *dramatic*. Particularly in regard to Keats' poetry has *spatial* been used as a critical term [by Tate]. For example, we might say that the structure of 'To Autumn' is *spatial*, not only because of the quality of the imagery, but because the structural elements exist, or coexist, in a relationship with each other which is different from the temporal progression that constitutes, on one level, all descriptive, narrative, and discursive writing. This *spatial* metaphor is applicable in more or less degree to any piece of writing in so far as it fulfills the formal conditions of art. It is by such considerations that we move in an ever widening circle away from the particular poem or experience, and the expressions which were initially metaphors thus tend to become abstract critical terms. 'To Autumn' itself, as we have seen, has implications about space and time, but because it scarcely takes the first step into metaphor, which is also a step toward statement, it is of all the odes at the farthest extreme from abstraction.)

We have observed the descriptive, temporal (course of day), and thematic aspects of the structure. Another aspect of structure appears when, once more, we consider the poem within the context of Keats' work. 'To Autumn' shares a feature of development with the odes on the Nightingale and the Grecian Urn. Each of these poems begins with presentation of realistic circumstances, then moves into an imagined realm, and ends with a return to the realistic. In 'Ode to a Nightingale', the most clearly dramatic of the poems, the speaker, hearing the song of the nightingale, wishes to fade with it 'into the forest dim' and to forget the painful realities of life. This wish is fulfilled in the fourth stanza – the speaker exclaims, 'Already with thee!' As the poem proceeds and while the imagined realm is maintained, the unpleasant realities come back into view. From the transition that begins with the desire for 'easeful Death' and through the references to 'hungry generations' and 'the sad heart of Ruth', the imagined and the real, the beautiful and the melancholy, are held balanced against each other. Then, on the word 'forlorn', the speaker turns away from the imagined, back to the real and his 'sole self'.

'Ode on a Grecian Urn' opens with an apostrophe to the actual urn. In the second stanza the imagined realm, the 'ditties of no tone', is invoked, and the 'leaf-fringed legend' comes to life. And here, too, the imagined life and real life are set in contrast against each other – the imagined is the negation of the real. It is in the fourth stanza that the imagined life is most fully developed and at the same time collapses into the real. The urn is left behind and the people are considered as not only in the scenes depicted on the urn, but as having left some little town. With the image of the town, desolate and silent, the imagination has completed its course. The people can never return to the town. In the final stanza they are again 'marble men and maidens' and the urn is a 'Cold Pastoral'. The statement about truth and beauty with which the poem ends is famous and much debated. It is conceivable that Keats is saying here what he has said elsewhere and in another way – in the *Ode* that begins

> Bards of Passion and of Mirth,
> Ye have left your souls on earth!
> Have ye souls in heaven too,
> Double-lived in regions new?

Toward the end of the poem there are these lines:

> Here, your earth-born souls still speak
> To mortals, of their little week;
> Of their sorrows and delights;
> Of their passions and their spites;
> Of their glory and their shame;
> What doth strengthen and what maim.
> Thus ye teach us, every day
> Wisdom, though fled far away.

Keats is not didactic here, nor does he claim didacticism for the bards. Their earth-born souls, their works, teach wisdom in speaking of the lives of men, and in bringing to men, generation after generation, an intensified awareness and thrill of being alive. It is the same wisdom which the urn will continue to teach 'in midst of other woe'. Keats believed that man's life, though rounded by a little sleep, is the stuff of which 'a thing of beauty' is made. Art takes its truth from life, and then returns it to life as beauty. The paradox that 'teases us out of thought' is that in a work of art there is a kind of life which is both dead and immortal. But, a melancholy truth, *only* the dead are immortal. If there is a heaven, Keats wanted it to be very much like earth, with a Mermaid Tavern where poets could browse 'with contented smack'. Delight is inseparable from melancholy because it is not conceivable apart from the mortal predicament. The answer to the question at the end of 'Ode to a Nightingale' – 'Do I wake or sleep?' – is, Both. In the structural imaginative arc of the poem, the speaker is returned to the 'drowsy numbness' wherein he is awake to his own mortal lot and no longer awake to the vision of beauty. Yet he knows that it is the same human melancholy which is in the beauty of the bird's 'plaintive anthem' and in the truth of his renewed depression. His way of stating this knowledge is to ask the question. Such considerations may clarify the truth-beauty passage. Whether they justify artistically Keats' use of these clichés of Platonic speculation is another matter. Keats was no Platonist, and if he had avoided those terms or if he had indicated more obviously, within the poem, that he was using the word *truth* in a sense close to the materialism of his own times, 'Ode on a Grecian Urn' would have had a different career in the history of literary criticism. It is unlikely that any amount of exegesis can rescue those last lines of the poem from associations with Platonic pietism, for Keats was not enough of a witty and conscious ironist to exploit successfully the philosophical ambiguities of *truth*. His romanticism was neither reactionary nor modernist in that way, and he may not even have been clearly aware of the ambiguity involved. If it could be proved that he was innocent of the ambiguity, and wanted only the philosophical prestige of the Platonic associations, then from his point of view the poem would not suffer from the difficulties which the merest sophistication can ascribe to it. Whether such ignorance of the law would be too outrageous to merit critical exoneration is a nice problem for critical theory.

In considering the arc of imagination as an aspect of structure, we have noticed that 'Ode to a Nightingale' approaches general statement and that 'Ode on a Grecian Urn' arrives at it. 'To Autumn' is obviously less explicit, although it shows the same structural aspect. The lush and realistic description of the first stanza is followed by the imagined picture of autumn as a person who, while a lovely part of a lively scene, is also intent upon destroying it. The personification is dropped in the final stanza, and there is again a realistic description, still beautiful but no longer lush, and suggesting an approaching bleakness.

The imaginative aspect of structure which the three odes have in common illustrates opinions which are in accord with the thought of Keats' times and which he occasionally expressed in his poetry. The romantic poets' preoccupation with nature is proverbial, and there are a number of studies (e.g., Caldwell's on Keats) relating their work and thought to the associationist psychology which was current in their times. According to this psychology, all complex ideas and all products of the imagination were, by the association of remembered sensations, evolved from sensory experiences. Keats found this doctrine interesting and important not because it led back to the mechanical functioning of the brain and the nervous system, but because sensations led to the imagination and finally to myth and poetry, and because the beauty of nature was thus allied with the beauty of art. In the early poem which begins, 'I stood tip-toe upon a little hill', Keats suggests that the legends of classical mythology were created by poets responding to the beauties of nature:

For what has made the sage or poet write
But the fair paradise of Nature's light?
In the calm grandeur of a sober line,
We see the waving of the mountain pine;
And when a tale is beautifully staid,
We feel the safety of a hawthorn glade:

While at our feet, the voice of crystal bubbles
Charms us at once away from all our troubles:

So that we feel uplifted from the world,
Walking upon the white clouds wreath'd and curl'd.
So felt he, who first told, how Psyche went
On the smooth wind to realms of wonderment.

What first inspired a bard of old to sing
Narcissus pining o'er the untainted spring?
In some delicious ramble, he had found
A little space, with boughs all woven round;
And in the midst of all, a clearer pool ...

In the *Ode to Psyche,* which was written during the same year as the other odes (1819),[1] Keats claims a similar experience for himself and contrasts it with those of the 'bards of old'. He has come upon Cupid and Psyche while he 'wandered in a forest thoughtlessly'. Although the times are 'too late for antique vows' and the 'fond believing lyre', he is still by his 'own eyes inspired'. If he cannot celebrate this symbolic deity with rites and shrine, then he proposes to do so with the service of the imagination, with 'the wreath'd trellis of a working brain, ... all the gardener Fancy e'er could feign' and with all that 'shadowy thought can win'. Conspicuous throughout Keats' work, blended and adjusted according to his own temperament and for his own purposes, are these *données* of his time: a theory of the imagination, the Romantic preoccupation with nature, and the refreshed literary tradition of classical mythology. These are reflected by the structure of his most successful poems, and are an element in their interrelatedness.

'To Autumn' is shorter than the other odes, and simpler on the surface in several respects. The nightingale sings of summer 'in full-throated ease', and the boughs in the flowery tale on the urn cannot shed their leaves 'nor ever bid the Spring adieu'. The world in which the longer odes have their setting is either young or in its prime, spring or summer. Consequently, in these poems some directness of statement and a greater complexity are necessary in order to develop the paradoxical theme, in order to penetrate deeply enough the temple of Delight and arrive at the sovran shrine of Melancholy. The urn's 'happy melodist' plays a song of spring, and the 'self-same song' of the nightingale is of summer. One of these songs has 'no tone', and the other is in either 'a vision or a waking dream', for the voice of the 'immortal Bird' is finally symbolized beyond the 'sensual ear'. But the music of autumn, the twittering of the swallows, remain realistic and literal, because the tensions of Keats's theme are implicit in the actual conditions of autumn, when beauty and melancholy are merging on the very surface of reality. Keats's genius was away from statement and toward description, and in autumn he had the natural symbol for his meanings. If 'To Autumn' is shorter than the other odes and less complex in its materials, it has the peculiar distinction of great compression achieved in simple terms.

SOURCE: *The Man in the Name: Essays on the Experience of Poetry*, Minneapolis, 1956.

NOTE

1. The Psyche, Melancholy, Nightingale, and Grecian Urn odes were written in May, and 'To Autumn' in September.

Kenneth Allott

THE 'ODE TO PSYCHE' (1958)

'To Psyche' is the Cinderella of Keats's great Odes, but it is hard to see why it should be so neglected, and at least two poets imply that the conventional treatment of the poem is shabby and undeserved. In his introduction to Keats (1895) Robert Bridges wrote of the 'extreme beauty' of the ode's last stanza and ranked the whole poem above 'On a Grecian Urn' (though not above 'On Melancholy')[1], and Mr T. S. Eliot in an unregarded parenthesis in *The Use of Poetry and the Use of Criticism* (1933) has commented more boldly, 'The Odes – especially perhaps the "Ode to Psyche" – are enough for his [Keats's] reputation'. I sympathize with these views. 'To Psyche' is neither unflawed nor the best of Odes, but to me it illustrates better than any other Keats's possession of poetic power in conjunction with what was for him an unusual artistic detachment – besides being a remarkable poem in its own right. This may be another way of saying that it is the most architectural of the Odes, as it is certainly the one that culminates most dramatically. Some of Keats's remarks about it are relevant here.

> The following Poem – the last I have written is the first and the only one with which I have taken even moderate pains. I have for the most part dash'd off my lines in a hurry. This I have done leisurely – I think it reads the more richly for it and will I hope encourage me to write other things in even a more peaceable and healthy spirit.[2]

Keats almost certainly wrote this before he wrote 'To a Nightingale', 'On a Grecian Urn' and 'On Melancholy', and it is possible that he felt later that these remaining Spring odes were written in a peaceable and healthy spirit. On balance this seems unlikely: 'To Autumn' is the only other ode one would expect him to characterize in these terms. The 'peaceable and healthy spirit' of 'To Psyche' can be explained by saying that Keats is more engaged as an artist and less directly engaged as a man in this poem (in spite of its superficial blemishes) than in 'To a Nightingale', and the unexpected degree of aesthetic distance is probably connected with his 'pains'. Those which can be subsumed under 'metrical preoccupation' have been fully discussed by Dr Garrod and later by Mr M. R. Ridley, but I suspect that Keats found a main difficulty in keeping his opulence from appearing obtrusive in what was for him a strain of unusually premeditated art. Apart from one or two lapses (mostly in the first stanza) I think he was successful – judged, that is to say, by the standards of success appropriate to the Odes, which involve a somewhat different kind of expectation, as Matthew Arnold knew, from that with which one would read *King Lear* or the *Agamemnon*.[3] What I feel very strongly is that 'To a Nightingale' should not be quoted to exemplify Keats's control of his poetic gift unless we are ready to disregard the difference between swimming powerfully but hypnotically with the tide of feeling and being able when necessary to make use of its force to come ashore roughly where one has planned. To change the metaphor, 'To a Nightingale' and 'On a Grecian Urn' have in common a pattern suggesting mounting sexual excitement and its relief – the point being that at an early stage in these poems the poet ceases to choose where he is going. This is not true of 'To Psyche', for which, as I have already said, an architectural metaphor seems best.

> Yes, I will be thy priest, and build a fane
>   In some untrodden region of my mind ...

The poem itself is a Corinthian detail in the 'fane' promised to the goddess. Possibly such considerations were in Mr Eliot's mind when he spoke of the ode: he may have felt, as I do, that Keats's artistry was more in evidence away from the empathic somnambulisms of the Urn and the Nightingale. Responsible critics of Keats such as Mr Middleton Murry and Sir Herbert Read might well dissent from this position and find the 'true voice of feeling' more distinctly in 'To a Nightingale' than in 'To Psyche'. Yet both these critics would probably agree that there is more detachment in the less-familiar ode, and it gives the poem a peculiar interest. Of course why 'To Psyche' should 'hit so hard'[4] is left unexplained by these remarks, and to understand how our feelings have been engaged we need to go much further into it. I say 'our feelings' because many readers seem to rise from the poem in the perplexed frame of mind honestly expressed by Mr Graham Hough in some sentences from his recent handbook, *The Romantic Poets* (1953).

> The *Ode to Psyche* seems ... the most purely fanciful of the Odes. It would be easy to take it as a lovely decorative mythology: but it is probably something more.[5]

Other readers must also have pondered the adequacy of Wordsworth's phrase for the invocation of Pan in *Endymion* ('A pretty piece of paganism') as a description of 'To Psyche', and felt with Mr Hough that it would not quite do. When Mr Hough tries to tell us what this 'something more' may be, he is less happy.

> ... the last stanza ... is not merely a piece of devotion to an obsolete myth; but a recognition by Keats that his own exploration is to be of the interior landscape, that his ultimate devotion is to be neither to the objective world, nor to any power outside himself.

I find the last stanza less confusing than this explanation of it, and I do not think its meaning can be stated so compendiously.

Before turning to my own analysis of 'To Psyche' I need to support the charge that the poem has suffered from being discussed in the course of scrutiny of the Odes as a group of poems whose interest is assumed to lie in one or other of two directions – either in the individual quality of the poems commonly regarded as the most important, or in the unique nature of some group-character which the critic is bent on discovering. In such contexts even the consideration of metrical form can be slanted unfavourably. For instance, it is generally agreed that Keats intended the irregular stanzas of 'To Psyche', with their inserted shorter lines, to produce loosely the effect of a 'Pindaric' ode, and it seems to me that this effect is obtained (the unrhyming lines are not much more noticeable than in 'Lycidas'). It is only if we become preoccupied with Keats's experiments with the sonnet-form in this ode – experiments which Messrs Garrod and Ridley have shown to be connected with the evolution of the stanza used in the other odes (a ten-line stanza except in 'To Autumn', which adds an eleventh line) – that we are likely to think that 'To Psyche' gives 'an uneasy impression of trying to be recurrent and failing'.[6] It does not in fact give such an impression unless we have stopped reading the poem as a poem and are looking at it instead as a stepping-stone to a later metrical perfection.

Most readers of 'To Psyche' will feel that they can safeguard their experience of the poem from a simple injustice of this sort, but a more insidious type of misunderstanding with a similar origin in the grouping of the Odes can be illustrated from Dr Garrod's account of the ode's last stanza. Keats has promised to serve Psyche as a priest and to dress a sanctuary for her in a corner of his mind. He concludes triumphantly and, I should have thought, unambiguously:

> And there shall be for thee all soft delight
> That shadowy thought can win,
> A bright torch, and a casement ope at night
> To let the warm Love in!

Psyche is in possession of the 'rosy sanctuary' and the torch is to direct her lover Cupid or Eros to her. The reference is, of course, to Cupid's visits by night in the legend as told by Apuleius (now that Psyche is deified and knows her lover for a god there is no further need for them to meet in darkness). The capital letter of 'Love' would seal this interpretation if there were any real doubt, and the human warmth of the quatrain may remind us that Keats was living next door to Fanny Brawne in April 1819 and probably kept an eye on her window when it was lit at night. Keats is vicariously gratifying a natural wish.

Dr Garrod reads the quatrain very differently.

> There shall be a 'bright torch' burning for her, and the casement shall be open to let her in at night. I do not find that any commentator has seized the significance of this symbolism. The open window and the lighted torch – they are to admit and attract the timorous *moth-goddess*, who symbolizes melancholic love . . . Keats has in fact identified the Psyche who is the soul (love's soul) with the Psyche which means moth.
>
> It is a strange goddess whom he has brought from her native unrealities into the reality of the imagination. But her identity is certain – we encounter her again, brought into darker shadow, in the *Ode on Melancholy*.[7]

I submit that this is a howler. Professor Finney and the late Ernest de Selincourt, however, describe it as a valuable comment, and more recently Mr John Holloway in his article on Keats's Odes in the *Cambridge Journal* (April 1952) implicitly approves of it when he borrows from Garrod to say of 'To Psyche',

'The stress falls largely on the melancholic aspects of Psyche the Love-goddess (she is called 'mournful Psyche' in *On Melancholy*)'. To all this the temperate reply is:

1. Psyche is not a goddess in 'On Melancholy'.
   In its context the plea 'Nor let the beetle, nor the death-moth be/Your mournful Psyche' is simply Keatsian for 'Do not let your soul be so mournful that all the most gloomy things you can think of (beetles, death-moths, etc.) become fit images for your mood'. It is clear that Keats knew that Psyche could mean both soul and butterfly (or moth), but there is no sign at all that he was thinking of Psyche, the woman or goddess of the legend. 'Veil'd Melancholy' is the only goddess in the poem.

2. There is no melancholy in 'To Psyche'.
   The nostalgia of the central section of the ode is a different emotion, and it is resolved comfortably in the last stanza with the indulged expectation of the re-enactment of Psyche's happiness. She is seen blissfully contented in the first stanza – neither timorous nor mournful. 'To Psyche' is a happy poem – in the sense of the expression, 'This is a happy ship', which does not mean that all personal problems have been solved for the crew.

What Dr Garrod is at is a rapid sleight-of-mind by which he first deceives himself and then others; and he is disposed to this error by the assumption that links of thought and feeling between the Odes must exist. There is certainly some truth in this assumption, but my example shows that it may be inexpedient to dwell on it.

Mr Holloway might have noticed Dr Garrod's mistake if it had not helped him to grind an axe of his own. Speaking empirically, the danger of 'general theories' of the Odes is that they encourage careless handling of the evidence, and, though Mr Holloway tries to be scrupulous, he pushes some of his evidence too far. I digress – and I think it will not prove to be a pointless digression – to deal with his suggestive argument because it has not been controverted, because I had to come to terms with it in my own attempt to read 'To Psyche', and because I believe that it could be restated in an acceptable form.

Mr Holloway holds that the Odes collectively are 'a psychological document ... of unique interest' because they 'prove to be a complex and detailed poetic revelation of what Keats knew himself as the creative mood', and he finds the main evidence for this view in certain repetitions of phrase which in his opinion establish a distinctive unity for the six poems (he includes 'On Indolence'). With the help of the *Letters* the creative mood of the Odes is then revealed as a drowsy, luxurious indolence, a visionary ecstasy in which consciousness struggles with insight on the very edge of oblivion. I object in reply that the value of the Odes as a 'psychological document' is questionable, that the poetic revelation of the nature of Keats's creative mood is not to be found in all the odes, or in any of them, perhaps, quite so clearly as Mr Holloway argues, and that in the sense in which it is to be found in several of the odes (including 'To Psyche') it is also to be found in much else of Keats's poetry. Mr Holloway claims both too much and too little. He claims too much in insisting that the Odes provide unambiguous psychological evidence – the 'creative mood' is partly a literary fabrication by Keats – and, again, in his assertion that his own viewpoint makes for 'a more sensitive, balanced, comprehensive interpretation of each poem by itself'. Here I merely note that it does not help with 'To Autumn' at all and that Mr Holloway nearly admits as much when he says that this poem 'may well have arisen from a quite independent poetic impulse'. He claims too little when he fails to see that in 'Sleep and Poetry', *Endymion*, 'Lamia' and 'The Fall of

Hyperion', for example, it is possible to discover with varying degrees of directness the same expectant passiveness in which pain and pleasure are relaxed neighbours (there are sexual overtones where sexuality is not overt). Mr Holloway has not looked far enough afield and he should have remembered an acute remark by Robert Graves: 'Keats's chief interest was the poet's relations with poetry, and the imagery he chose was predominantly sexual'.[8] The repetition of phrases from ode to ode is extremely interesting, but, if verbal correspondences are sought beyond the Odes, a few hours with a text and a concordance should convince the most sceptical that the accumulated evidence does not suggest an isolated character for the Odes: it shows, rather, how coherent and crammed with particulars – and, we must recognize, how inescapably literary – was Keats's poetic world throughout.

This brings me back to the 'psychological evidence' of the Odes. I am surprised that Mr Holloway should be so unsuspicious. Keats's extraordinary ability to assimilate to his own poetic needs whatever he picked up from his reading is a strong hint that the evidence may be doctored. For example, Mr Holloway argues that

> Surely I dreamt to-day, or did I see
> The winged Psyche with awaken'd eyes?

exemplifies the 'suspension between sleeping and waking' described in 'On Indolence', and he might have quoted a further corroborative echo from 'To a Nightingale':

> Was it a vision, or a waking dream?
> Fled is that music: – Do I wake or sleep?

Now this may be a circumstantial clue to the nature of Keats's creativeness, but it hardly seems possible to take it at its face value if we are aware that as an opening the quoted lines would be conventional (i.e.

without direct psychological significance) in an Elizabethan poem – see Spenser, *Amoretti* LXXVII:

> Was it a dreame, or did I see it playne
> a goodly table of pure yvory . . .

– or, more importantly, that Hazlitt had said in his *Lectures on the English Poets* (1818), some of which Keats had attended (he had read and weighed them all):

> Spenser was the poet of *our waking dreams*; and he has invented not only a language, but a music of his own for them . . . *lulling the senses into a deep oblivion* of the jarring noises of the world, from which we have no wish ever to be recalled.[9]

This is not an isolated example of a literary debt. Hazlitt touches several times in different lectures on various characteristics of the creative mood that Mr Holloway finds idiosyncratically projected in the Odes. I allow space for a further illustration, which suggests a literary element in Keats's Pleasure-Pain equivalence. He wrote:

> My heart aches, and a drowsy numbness pains
> My sense . . .
>
> 'Tis not through envy of thy happy lot
> But being too happy in thine happiness . . .[10]

and again:

> She dwells with Beauty – Beauty that must die;
> And Joy, whose hand is ever at his lips
> Bidding adieu; and aching Pleasure nigh . . .[11]

What he had heard Hazlitt say or had read in his printed lectures was this:

> The poetical impression of any object is that *uneasy, exquisite sense of beauty* ... that strives ... to relieve *the aching sense of pleasure* by expressing it in the boldest manner ...[12]

and, with reference to Milton, this (Keats would certainly pick up the echo of *Othello*):

> He refines on his descriptions of beauty; *loading sweets, till the sense aches* at them.[13]

II

If we try to forget the other odes and look at 'To Psyche' freshly, two immediate impressions seem normal. The first is that the poem opens badly but warms up rapidly after a weak start; the second is that, while the poem is a happy one, its tone is more exactly described if the happiness is thought of as defensive or defiant.

Robert Bridges observed that 'the beginning of this ode is not so good', and it needs no special insight to see that Keats could have produced a more arresting opening by deleting his first quatrain with its tasteless echo of 'Lycidas' and the displeasing phrase 'soft-conched ear' (Elizabethan for the cliché 'shell-like ear'). Again, later in the first stanza, the repetition of 'grass' in ll. 10 and 15 is clumsy, and the reader is nagged by the distracting survival of the rhymes for a further two lines after the sense has closed in:

> A brooklet, scarce espied.

Some of these faults probably came from working over the poem too often and at first, perhaps, too coolly – the price that Keats paid for his 'peaceable and healthy spirit' may have been that his 'pains' fixed his first stanza against further correction while its elements were still imperfectly combined (the version of the ode in the Pierpont Morgan Library, apparently the earliest that we have, is certainly not a first draft). Here the practical result is that several layers of composition appear to be cobbled together, not inexpertly, but without the ruthlessness of exclusion of otherwise acceptable phrase or rhyme that would have been given by a firm sense of poetic direction. The weakness disappears after the first stanza, which seems to confirm that Keats discovered his real subject in the process of writing – the rise in poetic temperature at the beginning of the third stanza ('O brightest! though too late for antique vows') may announce his full awareness of this discovery. I differ from Bridges about the value of this central section of the ode. He considers that the poem climbs with a steady improvement towards its conclusion and that its middle is only 'midway in excellence'. I find the first half of the third stanza at least the equal in excellence of the final stanza so admired by Bridges, particularly if his comment is kept in mind that 'the imagery is worked up to outface the idea' in the ode's last section. The observation has, of course, a wider and more general application to Keats's poetry – it is simplest to ascribe the 'outfacing' to his infatuation with a luxurious Elizabethan diction (as Lady Chatterley remarked to her husband, whom circumstances compelled to prefer Art to Life, 'The Elizabethans are so upholstered'). Against the overloaded imagery of the fourth stanza and some weak phrasing earlier, it is fair to set the successful rhyming. 'To a Nightingale', for example, has a bad rhyme in stanza six and forced expressions for the sake of rhyming in the first and last stanzas.

The other immediate impression, that of the Ode's defensive happiness, is not easy to pin down, but Keats seems to be rejoicing because of

> ... having to construct something
> Upon which to rejoice.

There is a defiant assertion that unaided he can put the clock back, that the ode itself proves that his is 'a fond believing lyre' in spite of an age

> ... so far retir'd
> From happy pieties ...

Positively, one relates this conviction to the nearness of Fanny Brawne – Keats is in love and for lovers 'happy pieties' are still possible.

In any move to go beyond these immediate impressions it is natural to examine carefully the serial letter to George and Georgiana Keats (Letter 123) in which an unrevised version of 'To Psyche' is copied out. It cannot, surely, be an accident that this copy of the ode should closely follow Keats's reflections on the world as a 'vale of Soul-making'. 'Do you not see', says Keats, 'how necessary a World of Pains and troubles is to school an Intelligence and make it a Soul?' We can hardly fail to link the intelligent 'Spark' struggling to become a soul as a result of a 'World of Pains and troubles' with the Psyche who achieves apotheosis and happiness after long wanderings and sufferings in search of Cupid. Keats had met the legend in Mrs Tighe's fantasticated Spenserian version as early as 1817, and he mentions Psyche's woes and her reward in 'I stood tip-toe' (ll. 141-50), but the reference to Apuleius in Letter 123 (see below) implies that by 1819 he had looked at a translation of *The Golden Ass*. For Keats the obvious translation was William Adlington's Elizabethan one of 1566, and C. L. Finney has noted verbal parallels between it and the ode.[14] Whether Keats's reflections on soul-making came directly out of his experience of life, and then, remembering that Psyche was the soul, he decided to read Apuleius in Adlington's version, or whether it was a reading of Adlington's account of Psyche's expiatory wanderings that prompted the famous description of soul-making in his letter, cannot be settled and perhaps is not very important. What can be shown convincingly is that the following passage was in his mind when he was writing 'To Psyche':

> Thus poore Psyches being left alone, weeping and trembling on the toppe of the rocke, was blowne by the gentle aire and of shrilling Zephyrus, and caried from the hill with a meek winde, which retained her garments up, and by little and little brought her downe into a deepe valley, where she was laid in *a bed of most sweet and fragrant flowers.*
>
> *Thus faire Psyches being sweetly couched among the soft and tender hearbs, as in a bed of sweet and fragrant floures,* and having qualified the thoughts and troubles of her restlesse mind, was now well reposed. And when she had refreshed her selfe sufficiently with sleepe, she rose with a more quiet and pacified minde, and fortuned to *espy a pleasant wood invironed with great and mighty trees. Shee espied likewise a running river as cleare as crystall:* in the midst of the wood well nigh at the fall of the river was a princely Edifice, wrought and builded not by the art or hand of man.[15]

Professor Finney asks us to set the italicised phrases beside the picture of Cupid and Psyche in the first stanza of the ode ('... couched side by side/In deepest grass ... where there ran/A brooklet, scarce espied: / Mid hush'd, cool-rooted flowers, fragrant-eyed ... They lay calm-breathing on the bedded grass ...'), but these verbal correspondences, though telling, are not more so than the way in which the landscape of Keats's fourth stanza reproduces the Apuleius-Adlington setting – in both descriptions a mountain wall and great trees shut off a flower-strewn valley containing a retreat or sanctuary. It also weighs a little with me that Adlington's '... she rose with a more quiet and pacified minde ...' seems to be crookedly echoed in a passage, already quoted, from Letter 123 ('... to write other things in even a more peaceable and healthy spirit ...').

How did Keats first hear of Apuleius? There can be no certainty, but Lemprière's *Classical Dictionary* (1788) may have been his source. It is certain that Keats referred to the dictionary – the entry under 'Psyche' is drawn on in his explanation of the ode in Letter 123. In Lemprière we are told that Psyche is 'a nymph whom Cupid married and conveyed to a place of bliss ... The word signifies *the soul*, and this personification of Psyche, first mentioned by Apuleius, is consequently posterior to the Augustan age, though it is connected with antient mythology ...', and again, a little below this, that Cupid's divinity 'was universally acknowledged, and vows, prayers, and sacrifices were daily offered to him'. Keats repeats some of the information for his brother and sister-in-law:

> You must recollect that Psyche was not embodied as a goddess before the time of Apulieus (*sic*) the Platonist who lived after the A[u]gustan age, and consequently was never worshipped or sacrificed to with any of the ancient fervour – and perhaps never thought of in the old religion – I am more orthodox that [*for* than] to let a heathen Goddess be so neglected.[16]

The similarity of these two accounts is less interesting than the differences between them. It is Keats who calls Apuleius a Platonist, which may strengthen the connection between 'To Psyche' and the reflections on soul-making. It is Keats, again, who puts together the two facts of Psyche's late personification and of the daily worship of Cupid in earlier times in order to insist in his letter that the goddess 'was never worshipped or sacrificed to with any of the ancient fervour'. Apparently this was what struck him most forcibly in Lemprière, so that the dull phrases of the dictionary may be said to govern the form taken by the ode's second stanza with its catalogue of imagined rites and devotions. 'This personification ... is consequently posterior to the Augustan age' is therefore the improbable germ of the apostrophe with which the second stanza opens:

> O latest born and loveliest vision far
> Of all Olympus' faded hierarchy! ...

Psyche is the 'loveliest vision far', lovelier than the Moon or Venus, because she is a love-goddess with an understanding of troubled human experience, because she has known in her own person – as no true Olympian could ever know – suffering and seemingly hopeless longing. She is 'loveliest' because she is 'latest' (there is much in 'Hyperion' and 'The Fall of Hyperion' obviously relevant to this identification) – not an early and therefore simple personification of such forces of nature as the wind or the sea, but a late and more sophisticated personification of human nature subjected to an inevitable and cruel process of growing up and growing old. The impatient dismissal of perfectibility ('... the nature of the world will not admit of it ...') with which Keats introduces his sermon on soul-making reveals the passion behind his perception that life is cruel and that to understand it is to be disenchanted. Man, he affirms, is 'destined to hardships and disquietude of some kind or other' (Tom had died of tuberculosis only four months earlier). It is this conviction, joined with his awareness of the existential pathos of the human soul (the tragic hero is any man, however fortunate), that makes the celebration of Psyche more than a piece of mythological embroidery; and in Psyche's final apotheosis there may be dimly expressed Keats's longing, which was now almost without hope, for some kind of personal immortality.

We need to be aware how closely ideas on the meaning and function of myth were bound up with Keats's attempt to make sense of the human situation. He tells George and Georgiana that his system of soul-making 'may have been the Parent of all the more palpable and personal Schemes of Redemption, among the Zoroastrians the Christians and the Hindoos'

(Letter 123). That is to say, in these intimate speculations Psyche has for him much the same degree of reality and unreality as 'their Christ their Oromanes and their Vishnu'. Figures drawn from religious myths – and to Keats Christianity was simply the last of the great mythologies – may be understood sympathetically, he thinks, as personifications of certain kinds of human need or self-knowledge (people 'must have the palpable and named Mediator and Saviour'). This is Keats's personal extension of a mode of mythological explanation then a commonplace. It has been conveniently summarised by Hazlitt.

> If we have once enjoyed the cool shade of a tree, and been lulled into a deep repose by the sound of a brook running at its foot, we are sure that whenever we can find a shady stream, we can enjoy the same pleasure again, so that when we imagine these objects, we can easily form a mystic personification of the friendly power that inhabits them, Dryad or Naiad, offering its cool fountain or its tempting shade. Hence the origin of the Grecian mythology.[17]

Keats first met these ideas powerfully in Book IV of Wordsworth's *The Excursion* (see, especially, ll. 847-87), a poem which in one mood he hailed as among the 'three things to rejoice at in this Age' (Letter 36). Though Wordsworth's influence on Keats's thought has not been fully traced – Book IV of *The Excursion* is quarry for much more in the Odes than is generally realized – it is, of course, accepted that Keats expounded Greek myths with a Wordsworthian accent in much of his early poetry, including *Endymion*.

Echoes of Milton's 'On the Morning of Christ's Nativity' have been noted in the second stanza of 'To Psyche'. De Selincourt, followed by Finney and others, cites the nineteenth stanza of the hymn:

> The Oracles are dumm,
> No voice or hideous humm

Runs through the arched roof in words deceiving.
Apollo from his shrine
Can no more divine,
With hollow shreik the steep of *Delphos* leaving
No nightly trance, or breathed spell,
Inspire's the pale-ey'd Priest from the prophetic cell ...

and finds a parallel in the ode's

No voice, no lute, no pipe, no incense sweet
From chain-swung censer teeming;
No shrine, no grove, no oracle, no heat
Of pale-mouth'd prophet dreaming.

This, however, does not quite do justice to Keats's memory. Milton's influence is active earlier in stanza two and also extends more subtly to the first half of the ode's third stanza. Thus one line from the twenty-first stanza of the hymn –

The *Lars*, and *Lemures* moan with midnight plaint...

– should be set beside Keats's

Nor virgin-choir to make delicious moan
Upon the midnight hours;

and Milton's two preceding lines –

In consecrated Earth,
And on the holy Hearth ...

– lend the force of 'consecrated' and 'holy', as applied to the elements of earth and fire, to reinforce 'haunted in his twentieth stanza:

From haunted spring, and dale
Edg'd with poplar pale,
The parting Genius is with sighing sent ...

– and so, I believe, help to inspire Keats's nostalgic

> When holy were the haunted forest boughs,
> Holy the air, the water, and the fire.

It is all much simpler than it sounds in the telling. Only three stanzas of Milton's hymn are involved and their splintering and telescoping in recollection suggest that Keats was not conscious of pastiche.

The chief Miltonic echoes have been recorded, but nobody has stopped to explain why Keats thought of Milton at this point in his poem. Clearly what happened was that 'faded' in l. 25 started a train of thought – to which a strong feeling-tone of regret was compulsively attached – about the end of the old Greek world with its 'happy pieties' (thought and feeling become explicit in the poem some ten lines later at the beginning of the third stanza). By literary association ideas of the fading of belief in the Olympian gods and of a lost numinous nature recalled Milton's description of the departure of the heathen deities of the Mediterranean world at the birth of Christ. The difference in tone between the two poems could hardly be wider. Milton writes at the end of heathendom with an almost fierce satisfaction (though it is certainly possible to detect an undercurrent of tenderness for the 'parting Genius' and 'Nimphs in twilight shade' of the classical world). Keats's tone is throughout one of unmixed regret for 'the fond believing lyre', for primitive times with their supposed simplicity and wholeheartedness of feeling. 'To Psyche' is now becoming something more than the celebration of a neglected goddess – it projects a nostalgia for an imagined wholeness of being once possible:

> Le squelette était invisible
> Au temps heureux le l'art païen –

but now, it would seem, impossible (except at lucky

moments for the poet and lover). The nostalgia has also a direct personal application. Keats's regret for the realm of Flora and old Pan is at the same time a regret for an earlier phase of his own mental growth before the disenchantment produced by reflection on a darkening experience of the world. A critic should move as delicately in these matters as if he were treading on eggshells, but this double reference is unmistakable. It would be an over-simplification to think of Keats's attitude as 'purely escapist'. By the spring of 1819 he was not trying to avoid thoughts of 'Whirlpools and volcanoes' – he had worked his way through at least to a theoretical acceptance of the value of heart-breaking experience: what he found hard to bear was that moments of joy and well-being should be poisoned by self-consciousness.

> The point at which Man may arrive is as far as the paral[l]el state in inanimate nature and no further – For instance suppose a rose to have sensation, it blooms on a beautiful morning it enjoys itself – but there comes a cold wind, a hot sun. – it cannot escape it, it cannot destroy its annoyances – they are as native to the world as itself.[18]

Men ought not to be less happy than roses, Keats might have said; and he believed that those who had – in a phrase from *Endymion* – 'culled Time's sweet first-fruits' had been able to live in the immediate present and were much to be envied. His own power to live in the present, which lay close to the sources of his poetry, depended for survival, as he knew, on his skill in preventing the withering of instinctive enjoyment by reflection.

If Keats thought that sun was exchanged for shadow at some necessary stage in the development both of the individual and human society as a whole, what was it on the universal plane that corresponded in his view to the over-balance of the reflective power that he feared in himself? The answer is to be found in

'Lamia' – the dangerous respect given to science (natural philosophy) at the expense of the imagination.

> Do not all charms fly
> At the mere touch of cold philosophy? ...
> Philosophy will clip an Angel's wings,
> Conquer all mysteries by rule and line,
> Empty the haunted air and gnomed mine –
> Unweave a rainbow ...[19]

It is known that this passage leans heavily on a paragraph in the first of Hazlitt's *Lectures on the English Poets*. The paragraph concludes:

> ... the history of religious and poetical enthusiasms is much the same; and both have received a sensible shock from the progress of the experimental philosophy.

Keats was less simple-minded than Hazlitt, but he accepted this judgement in essence. I do not think he was ever interested in discovering when this historical change had taken place or begun to take place; and, in saying so, I do not forget in how many ways he was a child of the Enlightenment or how mutually antagonistic were some of the 'prose' feelings with which he saluted the March of Mind. But Keats could not doubt that the poetic experience was valuable, or fail to suppose that in forgetting Pan men had lost something which they would not find in the *Transactions* of the Royal Society (the 'Fall' had taken place somewhere between the days of 'the fond believing lyre' and the present). He felt that currents of thought, among the most reputable and influential of his age, were inimical to the kind of poetry that he was writing and perhaps to all poetry; and that he needed to develop his resistance to their influence, and to the influence of the reflective traitor within himself, if he was to remain whole-hearted, i.e. keep his capacity for responding poetically to experience.

These ideas and feelings seem relevant to the fourth stanza of 'To Psyche'. Against the background that I have sketched the

> ... fane
> In some untrodden region of my mind

becomes the 'Great Good Place' where the experimental philosophy rumbles as harmlessly as distant thunder. Keats is constructing a mental landscape for whole-hearted enjoyment, and it is fitting that the scenery should recall the natural setting of the Pan festival in *Endymion* and 'Time's sweet first-fruits' under the side of Latmos. The similarity of setting can be shown by quotation

> Far, far around shall those dark-cluster'd trees
> Fledge the wild-ridged mountains steep by steep;
> And there by zephyrs, streams, and birds, and bees,
> The moss-lain Dryads shall be lull'd to sleep;
> And in the midst of this wide quietness
> A rosy sanctuary will I dress[20]

> Upon the sides of Latmos was outspread
> A mighty forest ...

> And it had gloomy shades, sequestered deep,
> Where no man went ...

> ... Paths there were many,
> Winding through palmy fern, and rushes fenny,
> And ivy banks; all leading pleasantly
> To a wide lawn, whence one could only see
> Stems thronging all around between the swell
> Of turf and slanting branches: who could tell
> The freshness of the space of heaven above,
> Edg'd round with dark tree tops? ...

> Full in the middle of this pleasantness
> There stood a marble altar, with a tress
> Of flowers budded newly ...[21]

In this 'green remote Cockaigne', which mixes the scenery of Latmos with the delectable valley in Apuleius, Keats will be able to preserve the visionary poetic experience from marauding analysis – the 'shadowy thought' expended for Psyche's delight is the gardener's creative reverie, opposed antithetically to the matter-of-fact operations of scientific logic. And Keats recognizes that keeping one part of the self simple and direct in its receptiveness is a matter intimately linked with the experience of love – the soul's sanctuary is rosy, Milton's 'celestial rosie red, love's proper hue'. We may note here that both the meeting of Cupid and Psyche in the first stanza and the description of the sanctuary in the fourth stanza have diffuse echoes of Spenser's Garden of Adonis (*Faerie Queene*, Bk. IV, Canto vi) and of the nuptial bower in Eden in *Paradise Lost*.

Since we have to do with a mental landscape, the introduction of Fancy as the gardener is apt enough (though it jars many readers at first). It follows easily as an idea from the Renaissance and neo-classic doctrine that fancy has the power of 'retaining, altering and compounding' the images supplied by the senses. The phrase quoted is from No. 411 of *The Spectator*, and in another paper Addison comes very close to thinking of fancy as a gardener when he says that the poet 'has the modelling of nature in his own hands' (No. 418). The same doctrine of art's ability to improve on nature may be found earlier in Sidney, Bacon and others; and Puttenham invents his own gardener:

> ... arte is not only an aide and coadiutor to nature in all her actions, but an alterer of them, and in some sort a surmounter of her skill, so as by meanes of it her owne effects shall appeare more beautifull or strange or miraculous ... the Gardiner by his arte will not onely make an herbe, or flowr, or fruite, come forth in his season without impediment, but will also embellish the same ... that nature of her selfe would never have done ...[22]

Puttenham, Sidney, Bacon and Addison express a stock idea – they are not, of course, in any sense sources of Keats's image, though I suspect that 'feign' in

> With all the gardener Fancy e'er could feign

may be a generalized Elizabethan echo. For example, Burton's discussion of Phantasy in *The Anatomy of Melancholy* mentions that it 'feigns infinite other unto himselfe' from the images furnished by daily experience. It is an amusing coincidence that Burton should choose 'Psyche's palace in Apuleius' as one example of fancy's power. I do not want to make too much of a last remark about 'the gardener Fancy', but I think it probable – since Fancy is the true creator of the mental landscape in this stanza – that Keats is glancing at the idea of God as the gardener who designed Eden. Indeed the association seems inevitable if we remember that Adam and Eve cull Time's first-fruits and that 'To Psyche' is about a kind of Fall.

If this attempt to understand 'To Psyche' is correct in outline, the poem moves through three stages. In the first stage (st. 1, ll. 1-23) Keats sets out to praise Psyche as the neglected goddess whose sufferings and mistakes represent the inevitable conditions of human experience. She has achieved 'identity' and lasting happiness. Love is her companion. Keats uses the convention of a sudden vision or waking dream, which comes to him when he is wandering 'thoughtlessly', because he had learned to speak in one breath of 'the most thoughtless and happiest moments of our Lives' (Letter 183), because Spenser's mythological poetry seemed to him a kind of waking dream, and because he knew that poetic experience was to be wooed by opening the mind receptively, not by concentrating its conscious powers. The vision of Psyche and 'the winged boy' in their Eden-like retreat draws some of its richness, as I have said, from descriptions of embowered lovers in Spenser and Milton. The tone of this first stanza is contented, even cool, except for the touch of feeling conveyed by the repetition 'O happy, happy dove', which measures the irksome distance between the actual world and the happiness that Psyche has already won.

The second stage of the poem spreads itself over the second and third stanza (ll. 24-49). Keats passes easily from the neglect of Psyche (born as a goddess too late for the fervours of primitive worship) to the fading and wearing-out of belief in the Olympians, and then to a nostalgic outpouring of feeling for the magnanimity of life when all nature was still 'holy' (full of the anthropologist's *mana*), all enjoyment wholehearted, and every herdsman or shepherd the poet of his own pleasure. The contrast is not with the age of Apuleius, but with a present which is a twilight for poetic and mythological modes of thought – the March of Mind has upset the balance of our natures, making the simple enjoyment of an experience in an 'eternal moment' an almost heroic achievement. Keats's regret embraces his own loss of an earlier innocence. After the first quatrain of the third stanza we have his defiance of these tendencies and changes in the age and in himself ('Yet even in these days ... I see, and sing, by my own eyes inspired'). At this point the repetition of the catalogue of worship from the ode's second stanza is a way of suggesting the poet's firmness or obstinacy. Psyche's worship will not be skimped or abbreviated by him in an age of unbelief.

The third and final stage of the poem consists of the fourth stanza (ll. 50-67). Here Keats gets his second wind. The movement introduced by the emphatic

> Yes, I will be thy priest ...

represents an accession of strength. The tread is more measured than in anything that has gone before, but there is no loss of smoothness or pace, and the whole stanza, consisting of a single long but quite coherent sentence, develops its momentum quietly at first, then confidently, and finally with exultation at its climax in the last quatrain. The defiance of the third stanza gives way to confidence as Keats comes to see how he can worship Psyche (the repetition of 'shall' and 'will' is extraordinarily positive). Briefly, he will do so by keeping 'some untrodden region' of his mind as a safe refuge where Psyche or the soul may unfold all her powers in a landscape and climate wholly benign and friendly. The stanza constructs the remoteness and peaceful seclusion of a valley:

> Far, far around shall those dark-cluster'd trees
> Fledge the wild-ridged mountains steep by steep;
> And there by zephyrs, streams, and birds, and bees,
> The moss-lain Dryads shall be lull'd to sleep.

The succession of pictorial details moves in and down from the dark mountains and forests to the humming warmth of the valley floor with its streams and pastoral drowsiness, and the description comes to a focus on Psyche's refuge or shrine:

> And in the midst of this wide quietness
> A rosy sanctuary will I dress ...

A complex image, accumulated from these details, is being offered as the equivalent of a mental state, which may be negatively defined by what it excludes. Calculation, anxiety and deliberate activity are shut out. The 'wide quietness' of the valley symbolizes a mood in which the soul will be able to breathe freely, and in which poetry, here defined as 'the wreath'd trellis of a working brain' may be coaxed to put forth its buds and bells and nameless stars. The soul is promised a rich indolence which will safeguard its natural gift for delight and restore to wholeness whatever the world beyond the mountains has broken down. In this luxurious sanctuary, a place made lovely and inviting with all the resources of a poetic imagination – and those resources are infinite, for Fancy

> ... breeding flowers, will never breed the same ...

– Psyche will be disposed to welcome the visits of love (whose 'soft delight' was still for Keats the soul's 'chief intensity'). Perhaps the final implications are that wholeheartedness can never be lost while Psyche is willing to welcome love at her casement, and, less directly, that love, poetry and indolence are the natural medicines of the soul against the living death it must expect from 'cold philosophy'.

SOURCE: *John Keats: A Reassessment,* ed. Kenneth Muir, Liverpool, 1958.

NOTES

1. *Collected Essays and Papers,* I.
2. *Letters,* ed. M. B. Forman (1935) p. 339.
3. See the conclusion to Arnold's essay on Keats in *Essays in Criticism,* second series (1888).
4. An expression borrowed from Robert Bridges.
5. Pp. 172-3.
6. Ridley, *Keats's Craftsmanship* (1933) p. 205.
7. *Keats* (1926) pp. 98-9.
8. *The Common Asphodel* (1949) p. 245.
9. Lecture II. My italics here and in the Hazlitt quotations below.
10. 'To a Nightingale'.
11. 'On Melancholy'.
12. Lecture I.
13. Lecture III.
14. *The Evolution of Keats's Poetry* (1936) II 614-15.
15. Finney's italics. Text from C. Whibley's reprint of the 1639 edition.
16. *Letters,* p. 340.
17. *Lectures on the English Poets,* lecture I.
18. *Letters,* p. 335.
19. Part II, ll. 229-30 and 234-47.
20. 'To Psyche', st. 4.
21. *Endymion,* bk. I, ll. 63-4, 65-6, 79-86, 89-91.
22. *The Arte of English Poesie,* lib. III, ch. XXV.

Kenneth Muir

THE MEANING OF THE ODES (1958)

A great deal has been written about the Odes, and some of it will be known to serious students of Keats's work – Robert Bridge's condensed judgements, Dr H. W. Garrod's account of the evolution of the stanza-forms used in the different odes, the subtle studies by Mr Middleton Murry and Professor Cleanth Brooks of the 'Ode on a Grecian Urn' and Professor William Empson's account of the 'Ode on Melancholy' may be mentioned – but there would seem to be room for a plain and elementary statement of what the odes are about. In this essay I shall deliberately avoid direct critical analysis.

Between the middle of February 1819, when he laid aside 'The Eve of St Mark', and the end of April, when he copied out the first of the Odes, Keats wrote very little verse; and it is apparent from several remarks in his letters that he did not fully realise that his indolence was a necessary pause before another period of creation. It was closely linked with the Negative Capability he felt to be a characteristic of the best poets, alternating moods of activity and indolence being, in fact, the rhythm of the mind necessary for the exercise of Negative Capability. It is arguable, indeed, that since during the act of creation the poet must organize, choose and reject, he can exercise Negative Capability only during his moods of receptive indolence – what Wordsworth called 'a wise passiveness'.

We can see from a passage in the long letter to George and Georgiana that, by overcoming the feverish desire for poetic fame and by ceasing to be obsessed with his love, Keats managed to see life more steadily: [1]

> Neither Poetry, nor Ambition, nor Love have any alertness of countenance as they pass by me: they seem rather like figures on a Greek vase – A Man and two women whom no one but myself could distinguish in their disguisement.

This passage is clearly the germ of the 'Ode on Indolence', though the poem may not have been written until a month or two later. Keats was wise to exclude this ode from the 1820 volume, because it is less highly wrought than the others, because the satirical tone of certain lines is out of key with the remainder of the poem, and because he had used some of its imagery elsewhere. He told[2] Miss Jeffrey that the thing he had 'most enjoyed this year had been writing an ode to Indolence'. 'The throstle's lay' links this ode to his own lines 'What the thrush said' and to Wordsworth's declaration that the blithe throstle was 'no mean preacher'. But the ode, like the letter, combines the praise of indolence with a repudiation of Love, Ambition and Poetry. Keats included in the same letter two sonnets in which he had attacked the desire for fame, and there were times when he seemed anxious to escape from the bondage of love – that is the apparent meaning of 'La Belle Dame Sans Merci'. In the 'Ode on a Grecian Urn', earthly passion is said to leave a cloyed heart, 'a burning forehead and a parching tongue'. In the 'Ode on Indolence' Keats seems to repudiate love altogether. But he was able to reject love, ambition and poetry only by satirizing them:

> For I would not be dieted with praise,
> A pet-lamb in a sentimental farce.

The uncertainty of tone is the result of his personal situation. He could acquire the means to marry only by earning fame as a poet. The praise of a wise passiveness is spoilt by the juxtaposition of the irritable attack on vulgarity. Keats should have written two separate poems.

In the same letter to George and Georgiana, Keats wrote his parable of the world as a vale of soul-making – an idea which was implicit in the third book of *Hyperion*. Near the end of the same letter he copied out 'La Belle Dame Sans Merci' and the sonnet on Paolo and Francesca, both based on the fifth canto of the *Inferno*, and both related, we may suppose, to his love for Fanny Brawne. Another sonnet, 'Why did I laugh tonight?', concludes with the thought that death is 'intenser' than life, that it is 'Life's high meed' – a thought which was to recur in the 'Ode to a Nightingale'.

In the weeks before the writing of the Odes we find that Keats was gradually realizing the creative function of indolence, he was anxious to achieve a state of non-attachment, and he was filled with a desire to find a meaning in human suffering so that his own and that of others could in some way be justified. He was torn between his continuing passion for Fanny and a wish to escape from the toils of ambition and love.

For an understanding of the Odes, however, it is necessary to go back a year, to the 'Epistle to Reynolds', written in March 1818. In the course of this poem Keats gives examples of the coherent and creative dreams – the waking dreams – enjoyed by the poet and the painter. One of these is the picture of the sacrifice, which was later to find a place on the Grecian Urn:

> Some Titian colours touch'd into real life, –
> The sacrifice goes on; the pontiff knife
> Gleams in the Sun, the milk-white heifer lows,
> The pipes go shrilly, the libation flows:
> A white sail shows above the green-head cliff,
> Moves round the point, and throws her anchor stiff;
> The mariners join hymn with those on land.

Another picture, based on Claude's 'Enchanted Castle', with 'windows as if latch'd by Fays and Elves' perhaps contributed to the 'magic casements' of the Nightingale ode. Keats goes on to express a wish that all our dreams might take their colours

> From something of material sublime,
> Rather than shadow our own soul's day-time
> In the dark void of night

that is, that they should mirror objective reality rather than the frustrations and inner conflicts of the dreamer. He confesses that he dare not yet philosophize, and doubts whether he will ever attain to the prize:

> High reason, and the love of good and ill.

Whether we read *love* or *lore* (words easily confused in Keats's handwriting) Mr Murry is probably right in thinking that the poet meant not the knowledge of good and evil, but rather a recognition that particular evil is universal good, an ability to see 'the balance of good and evil'. But Keats could not then make his experience of life fit a philosophical theory. Things – the problems of life – 'tease us out of thought', as the Urn, and Eternity, were to do. When the poet turns from the imaginary world of his creating to the actual world, his imagination is

> Lost in a sort of Purgatory blind.

He is dissatisfied with escapist poetry, and not strong enough to cope with the problems of good and evil. He convinces[3] his

> nerves that the world is full of Misery and Heartbreak, Pain, Sickness and Oppression.

The 'Chamber of Maiden Thought becomes gradually darken'd' and he feels the 'burden of the Mystery'. Such speculations inevitably interfere with the enjoyment of the present, so that in the Epistle Keats declares that

> It is a flaw
> In happiness, to see beyond our bourn, –
> It forces us in summer skies to mourn,
> It spoils the singing of the Nightingale.

At the end of the Nightingale ode the real world breaks in on the ecstasy of the bird's song.

In the concluding section of the Epistle we learn that the particular problem which was agitating Keats at this time was the struggle for survival in the animal kingdom – 'an eternal fierce destruction' symbolized not merely by shark and hawk, but by the Robin 'Ravening a worm'. When he came to write the Odes a year later the death of Tom had become for Keats the prime example of nature's cruelty. But we can see in the careless and disconnected thoughts of the Epistle that many of the themes treated in the Odes were already in his mind.

The first of the great Odes, 'To Psyche', – the first poem with which Keats had taken 'even moderate pains' – is, as Wordsworth said of another poem, 'a pretty piece of paganism'. Keats was apparently looking for a surrogate for religion. He speaks nostalgically of 'the fond believing lyre', and looks back to a pantheistic world when air, water and fire were holy. He is mainly concerned with the relationship between Psyche and Cupid. In becoming her priest he builds a fane where she can receive her lover – not as formerly in darkness, but with a bright torch. In other words Keats is proposing love as a substitute for religion; but, as Psyche is the soul, the poem may also be linked with his conception of the world as a vale of soul-making and with the deification of Apollo in *Hyperion*.

The 'Ode to a Nightingale' begins with a description of a man falling into a drugged sleep, so that it comes as something of a shock when we learn in the sixth line that the poet is 'too happy' in the happiness of the bird. This paradox is resolved in the sixth stanza in which Keats tells us that he has often 'been half in love with easeful death', and that in listening to the nightingale,

> Now more than ever seems it rich to die.

An easeful death was to Keats, who knew that Tom's fate might be his, 'a consummation devoutly to be wished'. In the third stanza his account of the miseries of life:

> Where youth grows pale, and spectre-thin, and dies

is also coloured by thoughts of Tom; and a link between Tom's illness and the nightingale is to be found in Keats's copy of Shakespeare. He read *King Lear* on 4 October 1818, a few weeks before Tom died, and he underlined the words 'Poor Tom' in Edgar's sentence:

> The foul fiend haunts poor Tom in the voice of the Nightingale.

Now, seven months later, when he heard an actual nightingale, Keats was haunted by Tom's ghost.

Keats, then, too happy in the happiness of the bird, dreams of escaping from the miseries of the world, first by a 'draught of vintage', and then 'on the viewless wings of Poesy'. The drink is to act, like the bird's song, as an opiate, allowing him to 'leave the world unseen'; and even in the richly sensuous evocation of the surrounding darkness we are reminded again of death in the phrase 'embalmed darkness' – an echo of the sonnet to sleep, death's counterfeit, the 'soft embalmer of the still midnight'. Now Keats toys with the idea of dying:

> To cease upon the midnight with no pain

with the bird singing his requiem.

Bridges complained of the illogicality of Stanza 7, since the nightingale, like man, is born for death. But the bird, unlike man, is not conscious of the hungry generations; and it is no more illogical for Keats to pretend that he is listening to the same bird as the one that sang to Ruth, than it was for Wordsworth to imagine he was listening to the same cuckoo he had heard in childhood, or for Rousseau to cry out when he saw the periwinkle. Hazlitt, indeed, referred in the peroration of one of his lectures to Wordsworth's lines to the Cuckoo, to Rousseau, and to Philomel;[4] Wordsworth's poem, like Keats's stanza, ends with a reference to faeryland; and it is significant that the reading of the draft 'perhaps the self-same voice' is nearer than that of the published text to Wordsworth's 'wandering voice ... A voice ... The same'. Another of Wordsworth's poems, 'The Solitary Reaper', may, as Mr Garrod has suggested,[5] 'by some obscure process of association', have contributed to the same stanza of Keats's ode. The 'solitary Highland Lass', reaping the corn and singing 'a melancholy strain', recalled Ruth standing 'in tears amid the alien corn'. Wordsworth mentions the nightingale and the cuckoo; like Keats he uses the epithet 'plaintive'; and in both poems the song fades away at the end.

But in any case the apparent illogicality of the stanza is transcended when the underlying symbolism is understood: the song of the bird is the song of the poet. Keats is contrasting the immortality of poetry with the mortality of the poet. He is saying with Horace, *Non omnis moriar*. This is the climax of the poem and the point where the different themes are harmonized – the beauty of the nightingale's song, the loveliness of the Spring night, the miseries of the world, the desire to escape from those miseries by death, by wine, or by poetry. Whereas when Keats wrote the Epistle to Reynolds the problems of life spoiled the singing of the nightingale, the song now acquired a greater poignancy from the miseries of the world.

The ode is not the expression of a single mood, but of a succession of moods. From being too happy in the happiness of the bird's song, Keats becomes aware of the contrast between the bird's apparent joy and the misery of the human condition, from the thought of which he can only momentarily escape by wine, by poetry, by the beauty of nature, or by the thought of death. In the seventh stanza the contrast is sharpened: the immortal bird, representing natural beauty as well as poetry, is set against the 'hungry generations' of mankind. The contrast is followed back into history and legend with Ruth in tears and the 'magic casements opening on the foam of perilous seas' – which, as in the Epistle to Reynolds, conceal a bitter struggle for survival. Even the faery lands are forlorn. Reality breaks in on the poetic dream and *tolls* the poet back to his self. Fancy, the muse of escape poetry, is a deceiving elf. Keats expresses with a maximum of intensity the desire to escape from reality, and yet he recognizes that no escape is possible.

One kind of mastery displayed by Keats in this ode is worth noting – the continuous shifting of view-point. We are transported from the poet in the garden to the bird in the trees; in the second stanza we have glimpses of Flora and Provence, followed by one of the poet drinking the wine; in the fourth stanza we are taken up into the starlit skies, and in the next we are back again in the flower-scented darkness. In the seventh stanza we range furthest in time and place, as we have seen; and in the last stanza we start again from the Hampstead garden, and then follow the nightingale as it disappears in the distance.

The 'Ode on a Grecian Urn' is dialectically opposed to the 'Ode to a Nightingale'. Keats in an earlier poem, 'Bards of Passion', had imagined that in heaven the nightingale sings

> divine melodious truth;
> Philosophic numbers smooth.

But in the ode, though the poet temporarily endows the nightingale's song with meaning, the bird is still 'a senseless, tranced thing'. We are left thinking that neither the beauty of nature nor the beauty of art can console us for the miseries of life. In the 'Ode on a Grecian Urn' Keats tries once more. The life of the figures on the urn possesses the beauty, the significance, and the externality of art; and this, in the third stanza explicitly, and throughout the poem implicitly, is contrasted with the transitoriness, the meaninglessness, and the unpoetic nature of actual life. The unwearied melodist,

> For ever piping songs for ever new; . . .

and the uncloying love of the imaginary world of the artist,

> All breathing human passion far above,

are contrasted with the inevitable imperfections of human existence. Yet the moral is not 'mortal beauty passes, but not that of art'. This interpretation ignores the development of the poem. In the last stanza Keats proclaims that the sorrows and the meaninglessness of life can be transcended if we learn the lesson of the Urn, that 'Beauty is Truth, Truth Beauty'. As early as November 1817 Keats had told Bailey[6] that he was

> certain of nothing but of the holiness of the Heart's affections and the truth of Imagination – what the imagination seizes as Beauty must be Truth – whether it existed before or not . . . The Imagination may be compared to Adam's dream He awoke and found it truth.

A month later he told his brothers:[7]

> The excellence of every art is its intensity, capable

> of making all disagreeables evaporate, from their being in close relationship with Beauty and Truth.

Now in the ode, as a result of the development of his mind during the earlier part of the year, Keats seems to go a stage further. The Urn is proclaiming that there is not merely a close relationship but an actual identity between beauty and truth. Whether the final words of the poem are supposed to be spoken by the Urn or whether they are intended to be the poet's own comment does not greatly affect the meaning. The words –

> That is all
> Ye know on earth, and all ye need to know –

are dramatically appropriate. Momentarily, and in response to the beauty of the Urn, the poet can accept the proposition – a natural development of his own earlier aphorisms – that beauty is an image of truth, and that therefore, if we see life steadily and see it whole, the disagreeables will evaporate as they do in a great work of art. Keats seems to protect himself from the criticism of common-sense by leaving it doubtful whether his own views are to be identified with those of the Urn. Art claims that life could be as meaningful as art. When we are experiencing a work of art we are prepared to give our assent, though at other times we may be sceptical.

Keats was aware, as Yeats was aware when he sailed to Byzantium, of the limitations of art. Even when he is congratulating the lover on the permanence of his unsatisfied love, he hankers after 'breathing human passion'; and when he is describing the scene of sacrifice which will remain for ever beautiful, he thinks of the desolate town, emptied for ever of its inhabitants. Art is invaded by human suffering. The cold pastoral, although perfect, is lacking in the warmth of reality. It is this undertone which prevents us from branding the message of the Urn as irresponsible, or 'uneducated', or 'intrusively didactic'.

The 'Ode on Melancholy' has links with several of the other odes. Keats had proposed to honour Psyche by making 'a moan upon the midnight hours', and his fane would have 'thoughts, new grown with pleasant pain'. The song of the nightingale had made him too happy, his heart aching, and his senses pained by a drowsy numbness. There is a strain of melancholy, as we have seen, in the fourth stanza of the 'Ode on a Grecian Urn'. Keats, moreover, had written some verses on the juxtaposition of joy and sorrow in the previous year:[8]

> Welcome joy, and welcome sorrow,
> Lethe's weed and Hermes' feather ...
> Infant playing with a skull ...
> Nightshade with the woodbine kissing ...
> Oh! the sweetness of the pain!
> ... let me slake
> All my thirst for sweet heart-ache!
> Let my bower be of yew,
> Interwreath'd with myrtles new.

Now in the first stanza of the 'Ode on Melancholy' Keats introduces *Lethe, nightshade* and *yew*, but he rejects them as being unnecessary means of arousing melancholy. He likewise rejects the stock properties – the skull, the gibbet and the phantomship – mentioned in a deleted stanza which had been partly derived from Burton's *Anatomy of Melancholy*.[9]

> This terrour is most usually caused, as *Plutarch* will have, *from some imminent danger, when a terrible object is at hand* ... *by the sudden sight of some spectrum or devill* ... the sight of a monster, a *carcase* ... where a *coarse* hath been ... with a *dead man* ... At *Basil* ... where a malefactor hung in *gibbets*.

Horrors of this kind, and even the beetle, the death-moth, and the owl, are not only unnecessary as a means of arousing melancholy, they are to be shunned since they 'drown the wakeful anguish of the soul' and prevent us from experiencing to the full the subtler melancholy of which Keats is writing. Melancholy is to be sought in beauty and joy – in a rose, a rainbow, or the anger of a mistress. Because beauty is transient, because love and joy fade, enjoyment must be accompanied with melancholy. Beauty is lovely because it dies and impermanence is the essence of joy; so that only those who are exquisitely sensuous and able to relish the finest joys can behold the 'Veil'd Melancholy':

> She dwells with Beauty – Beauty that must die;
> And Joy, whose hand is ever at his lips
> Bidding adieu; and aching Pleasure nigh ...
> Ay, in the very temple of delight
> Veil'd Melancholy has her sovran shrine,
> Though seen of none save him whose strenuous tongue
> Can burst Joy's grape against his palate fine,
> His soul shall taste the sadness of her might,
> And be among her cloudy trophies hung.

Keats is really writing about the poetical character. The fine sensitivity necessary for the writing of poetry makes the poet vulnerable both to joy and sorrow. The realization that love and beauty are subject to time intensifies his joy in them, as we can see from Keats's own poems or Shakespeare's *Sonnets*.

This ode is not quite perfect. The last three lines of the second stanza exhibit both the awkwardness that is apt to beset Keats when he is writing of women and also the lapses he is led into by the need to find a rhyme. It is difficult otherwise to explain 'let her rave'. The beautiful image at the beginning of the same stanza has been criticized for its irrelevance. The 'weeping cloud' and the 'April shroud' are admirable; but the information that the rain 'fosters the droop-headed flowers all' suggests, what Keats presumably did not intend, that the melancholy fit is creative.

'To Autumn', the last of the odes, requires little commentary. Keats's own account of the writing of the poem gives us a good idea of its theme:[10]

> How beautiful the season is now – How fine the air. A temperate sharpness about it. Really, without joking, chaste weather – Dian skies – I never lik'd stubble-fields so much as now – Aye better than the chilly green of the Spring. Somehow a stubble-plain looks warm – This struck me so much in my Sunday's walk that I composed upon it.

Keats describes Nature as she is. He was in this like Peter Bell:

> A primrose by a river's brim
> A yellow primrose was to him,
> And it was nothing more.

'To Autumn' expresses the essence of the season, but it draws no lesson, no overt comparison with human life.[11] Keats was being neither allegorical, nor Wordsworthian. Goethe once remarked[12] that

> for most men the vision of the pure phenomenon is not enough, they insist on going further, like children who peep in a mirror and then turn it round to see what is on the other side.

Keats in this poem is almost content with the pure phenomenon.

SOURCE: *John Keats: A Reassessment*, ed. Kenneth Muir, Liverpool, 1958.

NOTES

1. *Letters*, p. 315.
2. Op. cit., p. 347.
3. Op. cit., p. 144.
4. See the discussion in *John Keats: A Reassessment*, ed. Kenneth Muir (1958) p. 145.
5. *Keats* (1926) p. 111.
6. *Letters*, p. 67.
7. Op. cit., p. 71.
8. *Poems*, ed. de Selincourt, p. 256.
9. Part 1. See 2, mem. 4. subs. 3.
10. *Letters*, p. 384.
11. But see the essay in *John Keats: A Reassessment*, p. 95.
12. The passage was quoted by J. M. Murry.

SELECT BIBLIOGRAPHY

J. R. MacGillivray, *Keats: A Bibliography and Reference Guide, with an Essay on Keats's Reputation* (University of Toronto Press, 1949; Oxford U.P., 1949). This first-rate bibliography, of editions of the poems and letters and of biographical and critical studies, is an indispensable tool for anybody who wants to follow seriously the growth of Keats's reputation.

John Keats, *The Letters of Keats, 1814-1821*, ed. Edward Hyder Rollins, 2 vols (Harvard U.P., 1956; Cambridge U.P., 1958). Professor Hyder Rollins died in the year of the publication of this great edition, the climax of a life devoted to Keats scholarship. In completeness, accuracy and thoroughness of annotation and indexing it supersedes all earlier editions of the letters. Keats in his letters tells us more about what it is like to be a poet, and more about his fundamental poetic thinking, than any other English poet has told us in such an informal and delightful way. The letters, in spite of all the excellent subsequent work of many critics and biographers, remain the best companion to the poems.

Matthew Arnold, *Essays in Criticism*, second series (Macmillan, 1888). Arnold died in 1888, so this is a posthumous publication. The whole of the essay on Keats, of which only a short extract is printed here, should be read. Arnold saw Keats as the one really dedicated *artist* among the romantics and praised also the vigour and elevation of his poetic thinking and the manly courage of his character.

A. C. Swinburne, *Miscellanies* (Chatto & Windus, 1886). Swinburne's criticism today is, even more than his poetry, neglected. Like the poetry it could be shrill, diffuse, and could lose its balance, because Swinburne had a deep inner need both to praise and blame, in a tone nearing hysteria. Nevertheless, the essay on Keats here, originally written for the *Encyclopaedia Britannica*, is a masterpiece. Swinburne is the first critic to give the odes a central position in Keats's work, and to emphasise Keats's 'Shakespearean' quality. His relative placing of the other poems, and his sense of the extraordinary progress made by Keats between his first and second and even more strikingly between his second and third volumes, coincides remarkably closely with the general verdict of twentieth-century criticism.

Amy Lowell, *John Keats*, 2 vols (Houghton Mifflin, 1925; Cape, 1925). An eccentric but energetic member of a great American literary family (James Russell Lowell, Amy Lowell, Robert Lowell), herself an uneven but influential poetess (she converted Ezra Pound's 'Imagism' into what he called 'Amygism'), Miss Lowell wrote a biography which has been superseded as a scholarly work but which is still worth reading for its fire and enthusiasm and for its pioneer effort to relate the order of composition of the poems to the details of Keats's life.

Claude L. Finney, *The Evolution of Keats's Poetry*, 2 vols (Russell, 1936). Robert Gittings, in his preface to his excellent recent biography of Keats, *John Keats* (Heinemann, 1968), writes: 'In the past thirty years, three great scholarly critical biographies of John Keats have appeared, the works of Professor C. L. Finney, W. J. Bate and Aileen Ward.'

M. R. Ridley, *Keats's Craftsmanship* (Clarendon Press, 1933; reprinted Methuen, 1963, Russell, 1962). Deriving partly from H. W. Garrod's study, but improving on it, this is still the best study of Keats's manuscript revisions and of the manner in which the stanza forms of the odes derived from Keats's fascination with, and dissatisfaction with his own achievement in, the various English forms of the sonnet.

F. R. Leavis, *Revaluation: Tradition and Development in English Poetry* (Chatto & Windus, 1936; paperback eds by Penguin, 1963, and Norton, 1963). Dr Leavis is the *doyen* of living English critics, and in his lifetime this book has become a classic, though a controversial one. The chapter on Keats is particularly distinguished and concentrates, illuminatingly, on the odes.

Earl R. Wasserman, *The Finer Tone: Keats's Major Poems* (Johns Hopkins Press, 1953; Oxford U.P., 1953). Hard reading, because of its very detailed and laborious linguistic and metaphysical analysis, this book contains the lengthiest, and in detail perhaps the most sensitive, study of the odes that has yet been written. More suitable for graduate students, however, than for sixth-formers or undergraduates.

Aileen Ward, *John Keats: The Making of a Poet* (Viking Press, 1963; Secker & Warburg, 1963). This is probably the most readable of all modern critical lives of Keats. Professor Ward absorbs her exact and detailed scholarship into the texture of a rapid, sensitive narrative, so that the reader sometimes feels almost that he is reading a great novel. Keats as a man perhaps comes more vividly alive here than in any other biographical study.

Walter Jackson Bate, *John Keats* (Harvard U.P., 1963;

Oxford U.P., 1963; Oxford paperback ed., 1967). The standard modern critical biography. Less exciting to read than Miss Ward's book, since the method is one of objective scholarship rather than of imaginative identification through scholarship, this is nevertheless a very sane and sympathetic study of the man combined with a balanced estimate of the poems. The chapters on the composition and meaning of the odes are extremely sensitive and thorough.

Ian Jack, *Keats and the Mirror of Art* (Oxford U.P., 1967). A fascinating account of the influence of the visual arts on Keats's poetry. Photographs are included of the various urns which Keats may have had in mind when composing 'Urn'.

Robert Gittings, *John Keats* (Heinemann, 1968). This most recent biography is worthy to rank with those of Finney, Ward, and Bate. 'What', Mr Gittings asks, 'is there to say that they have not already said? The answer is to be found in one of the most curious paradoxes of literary history. For various reasons, the greater part of what Keats's hand put on paper, manuscripts of poems, letters, marginalia, is now in the United States of America, and readily available to anyone resident there. Yet the evidence for most of the facts of his life, and even more, the living origin of much of his work, remains in England, not easily available to American scholars, except on a prolonged visit, since it requires close research in public, local and private collections. Thanks to advantages, which I have gratefully acknowledged elsewhere. I have enjoyed the best of both these worlds....'

Gittings's *The Odes of Keats and their earliest known Manuscripts* (Heinemann, 1971), with its very useful facsimile reproductions, appeared too late to be made use of in this volume.

James Dickie, *The Grecian Urn: An Archaeological Approach* (John Rylands Library, Manchester, 1969). This is a remarkably interesting pamphlet which seeks sources for the scenes depicted on Keats's Grecian urn in the Sosibios vase in the Musée Napoléon (or rather on a not wholly accurate plate of this, from which Keats made a tracing, in a book published in 1814), in the Borghese vase, the Holland House vase, the Towneley vase, or reproductions of these. Dr Dickie relates Keats's sensuousness in the odes to his precise and educated feeling for the plastic arts.

NOTES ON CONTRIBUTORS

KENNETH ALLOTT (1912–73); poet and critic, he was Professor of English Literature in the University of Liverpool, co-editor (with Geoffrey Grigson) of *New Verse* and editor of the Penguin anthology, *Contemporary Verse*. His *Collected Poems* were published in 1975.

CLEANTH BROOKS: born 1906; Emeritus Professor of Rhetoric at Yale. His important critical studies include *Modern Poetry and the Tradition* (1939), *The Well-Wrought Urn* (1947) and his study of William Faulkner (1978).

KENNETH BURKE: born 1897; poet, novelist and critic, by some regarded as the American equivalent of William Empson. His publications in critical theory include *The Philosophy of Literary Forms* (1941; 3rd edn 1974), *A Grammar of Motives* (1945), *A Rhetoric of Motives* (1950), *Language as Symbolic Action* (1966) and *Dramatism and Development* (1972). His *Collected Poems, 1915–1967* were published in 1968.

T. S. ELIOT (1888–1965): poet, critic and playwright.

WILLIAM EMPSON (1906–84): poet and critic, he was Professor of English, University of Sheffield (1953–71) and Honorary Fellow of Magdalene College, Cambridge. His influential critical studies include *Seven Types of Ambiguity* (1930), *Some Versions of Pastoral* (1935), *The Structure of Complex Words* (1951) and *Milton's God* (1961). The revised edition of his *Collected Poems* was published in 1961.

H. W. GARROD (1878–1960): a Fellow of Merton College, Oxford, and (1923–8) Professor of Poetry in Oxford. His publications include *Keats* (1926) and an edition of Keats's poetical works (1929) which was the standard modern text until publication (1970, 1972) of Miriam Allott's edition.

JOHN HOLLOWAY: born 1920; poet and critic, Professor of Modern English at Cambridge (1972–84). his publications include *The Victorian Sage* (1953), *The Charted Mirror* (1960), *Widening Horizons in English Verse* (1966), *Narative and Structure* (1979) and studies of Shakespeare's tragedies and of Blake.

KENNETH MUIR: born 1907; King Alfred Professor of English Literature, Liverpool University (1951–74); editor of *Shakespeare Survey* (1965–79), of the New Arden editions of *Macbeth*, *King Lear*, and of the

Casebook on *The Winter's Tale*. His other publications include, in addition to his study of Keats and writings on Wyatt, *Shakespeare and the Tragic Pattern* (1959), *Shakespeare's Tragic Sequence* (1972), *The Sources of Shakespeare* (1977) and *Shakespeare's Comic Sequence* (1979).

SIR ARTHUR QUILLER-COUCH (1863–1944); critic and novelist, and the first King Edward VII Professor of English Literature at Cambridge (1912-44).

I. A. RICHARDS (1893–1979): poet and critic, he taught at Cambridge and Harvard. *Principles of Literary Criticism* (1924) and *Practical Criticism* (1929) have exerted a strong influence on the study of literature. His *New and Selected Poems* appeared in 1978.

M. R. RIDLEY: sometime Lecturer in English, Bedford College, University of London; his publications include *Keats's Craftsmanship* (1933) and the New Arden editions of *Antony and Cleopatra* (1953) and *Othello* (1957).

G. ST QUINTIN: literary scholar.

ALLEN TATE (1899–1979): American poet, novelist and critic, he taught at several universities and latterly at Minnesota. A distinguished member of 'The Fugitives' group of American Southern writers, his publications include *On the Limits of Poetry* (1948), *The Man of Letters in the Modern World* (1956), *Collected Essays* (1959) and *Essays of Four Decades* (1969). His *Collected Poems* appeared in 1977.

LEONARD UNGER: born 1916; American critic and scholar, formerly Professor of English, University of Minnesota. His publications include *The Man in the Name* (1956; reprinted 1974), studies of Donne and T. S. Eliot, and the edited volume, *Seven Modern American Poets: An Introduction* (1967).

ALVIN WHITLEY: American literary scholar.

INDEX

Keats himself and the odes individually are not indexed. References to other poems of Keats, other works by other writers, and persons contributing to or mentioned in the text are confined to those which have direct relevance to the critical commentaries.